Honoring the Doughboys

FOLLOWING MY GRANDFATHER'S WORLD WAR I DIARY

Photographs and text by

Jeffrey A. Lowdermilk

with a foreword by Helen Patton

George F. Thompson Publishing

To my Mother,

Joyce Carlson Lowdermilk,

July 5, 1926 – December 2, 2011

Contents

Foreword

Helen Patton, granddaughter of General George S. Patton, Jr. taken at her second home in Nehou, Normandy, France.

WHEN I WAS A LITTLE GIRL, my father, who would later become another General Patton, would lead my siblings and me by the hand through the villages and plains of the Meuse-Argonne. Throughout our tour, he would point out with constant wonder the freshness of the pockmarks on the land from World War I.

There was always an urgency to his words. He begged us, little as we were, to fathom the brutality that took place there. At the Ossuaire de Douaumont near Verdun, he told us, "Kids, just look at the tips of those bayonets coming out of the dirt! And the huge glass containers of nothing but young men's bones. Those men didn't stand a chance!"

A few years ago, the world said goodbye to the last known veteran of the Great War. Now, as veterans of World War II and the Korean War prepare to give their final salute, we quake to think that the memories of these heroes could be lost. The urgency welling up in us borders on panic. We cling to stories of our veterans, fearing that their memories will fade with their passing, and that no one will remember the bayonets.

We do not wish to hinder the progress of time, which inevitably will cover all marks of the Great War with the earth and grass. Instead, we celebrate the efforts of one veteran's grandson, who was moved enough to make this journey of remembrance for us. He takes us by the hand through the grass and muddy plains and shares with us his photographs inspired by personal reflections of the *then and there* as well as the *here and now.*

Thank you, Jeff, for this labor of love.

—HELEN PATTON

"What place is this? Where are we now? I am the grass. Let me work."

– CARL SANDBURG, "GRASS"[1]

Opposite: The French people always include their children in their World War I commemoration ceremonies. These school children were at the ninetieth anniversary ceremony of the Meuse-Argonne Offensive in the village of Neuvilly-en-Argonne.

" Time will not dim the glory of their deeds ." General John J. Pershing

George A. Carlson
353rd Infantry Regiment
89th Division
Denver, Colorado USA

Jeffrey A. Lowdermilk
Grandson - Photographer
Santa Fe, New Mexico USA

Granddad's portrait (left) was taken in Prüm, Germany, during the Allied occupation. He was twenty-four years old at the time. I took my portrait with a tripod on the steps of the church in Stenay, France, in November 2005. Granddad and his company were the first U.S. troops into Stenay on the morning of the Armistice, November 11, 1918.

Preface

This book is about following the World War I diary of my grandfather, George A. Carlson, who was a doughboy, a member of the American Expeditionary Forces, during World War I. I have traveled in his footsteps throughout Europe many times now, photographing and keeping my own journal of experiences and emotions as I traveled to the places where my grandfather fought so long ago. My goal, as much as possible, has been to bring his diary to life. With my heart and spirit, I followed his path through France, Belgium, Luxembourg, and into Germany. The book chronicles his wartime experiences, but it also highlights my own life-enriching journey of discovery and the friends I made along the way. These collective experiences are my grandfather's posthumous gifts to me.

Granddad was from Denver, Colorado, and he returned home after the war to live a full life. He almost made it to his ninetieth birthday. I was thirty-two years old when he passed away. He was an extremely influential person in my life, teaching me the importance of service and showing me that dedication to this ideal is one of the most commendable of all virtues. His kindness, cheerfulness, and dedication to helping others have served as inspirations for how to live my life.

The paramount thing I have learned about America's World War I soldiers is that, despite their incredible service to humankind, time *has* "[dimmed] the glory of their deeds." The United States was forced into a European conflict that, at the time, 1914–1918, was the most horrific war in all of human history. In the words of Winston Churchill, from his book, *World Crisis, 1923–1931*:

> To fight in defense of his native land is the first duty of the citizen. But to fight in defense of someone else's land is a different proposition. . . . To cross the ocean and fight for strangers, far from home, upon an issue the making of which one has no say, requires a wide outlook upon human affairs and a sense of world responsibility.[3]

"Time will not dim the glory of their deeds."
— General John J. Pershing[2]

The United States entered the war during the late stages to help its allies, France and Great Britain, defeat Germany, which, under the dictatorship of Kaiser Wilhelm II, threatened to dominate Europe. America's herculean efforts tipped the balance in favor of the Allies and laid the geopolitical foundation for the twentieth century by saving freedom and preserving democracy in western Europe. At the time of the Armistice (cease-fire) on November 11, 1918, 2,000,000 American soldiers were on the front lines in France and Belgium. The courage, determination, and sacrifice of these soldiers made the difference in this titanic struggle. Nevertheless, their memory is sliding into the forgotten past. The purpose of this book is to shine the light of awareness and gratitude on these heroes.

Although the American Civil War predates America's entry into World War I by sixty-six years, the average American's awareness of it seems stronger than that of World War I, because it happened on our own soil. The Civil War is ingrained in our national psyche, and its battlefields—now national and state parks and monuments—scatter the landscape. It would be fair to say that most educated Americans are knowledgeable about President Abraham Lincoln, Generals Ulysses S. Grant, and General Robert E. Lee; the valor of Pickett's Charge at Gettysburg, the horrendous loss of life at Antietam, and the Confederate Army's surrender at Appomattox Court House. But how would the same Americans do if asked about President Woodrow Wilson, Kaiser Wilhelm II, General John J. Pershing, Marshal Ferdinand Foch, Field Marshal Douglas Haig, the valor of the U.S. Marine Corps at Belleau Wood, the U.S. Army's first tank battle in the Saint-Mihiel Offensive, the definitive Battle of the Meuse-Argonne, or the Armistice? Just as the Civil War has its monuments, there are also American World War I cemeteries and monuments in Europe, all of which are administrated by the American Battle Monuments Commission (ABMC), but the existence of which are unknown to many Americans. More information about the ABMC may be found in Appendix A. This book aims to honor and remember the heroes whom these monuments commemorate and to provide the means by which we may connect with our forefathers, our heritage, and our values as a nation.

An article in *The Economist* stated that some 25,000 books and articles have been written on World War I.[4] Therefore, it is not my intention here to write yet another history of The Great War. Rather, I have chosen to tell the story of one man, my grandfather, and to share my experiences following in his footsteps, with enough background history to support the information contained in his diary. My hope in so doing is to illuminate the experiences of the doughboys—and to inspire you to read more of those thousands of books.

French doughboy re-enactor with an American Flag at the ninetieth anniversary ceremony of the Saint-Mihiel Offensive (September 13, 2008), Fliery, France.

Introduction
Granddad's Stories

"WE STAYED UP ALL NIGHT and talked, because we knew in the morning we would all be killed," Granddad said with a somber face. I was a ten-year-old and sat wide-eyed on the sofa as Granddad told me his Armistice Day story for the first time.

He went on: "It was the evening of November 10, and we were camped near the old train station on the west side of the Meuse River. On the other side of the river was the town of Stenay, and our orders were to attack Stenay in the morning. When the Germans retreated, they dynamited the bridge, so huge blocks of concrete were scattered in the river. The only way across was to pick our way from block to block, and we knew there was a German machine gun in every window of the town pointed at the demolished bridge."

Growing up in Denver, Colorado, I spent a good deal of my youth at my maternal grandparents' house, which was only a few miles from where we lived. My grandfather loved to tell his enchanting stories, and I loved to listen. We made a very good team. I'm sure I developed my love of history from listening to his stories.

Through the years, Granddad told me stories of his family's history. His father, Johann Alfred, immigrated to America from Sweden during the mid-1880s. He had grown up on the family farm near the village of Holm on Sweden's southwestern coast. He was the youngest son in a culture where the oldest son would inherit the farm. Outside work and future prospects were as scarce as the food. So, at the age of eighteen, he left home to stake his future in America. He would never see his parents or his homeland again. He made the long sea voyage in a ship crowded with other Swedes in search of a better chance at life. Granddad told me that the first steady job his father had was at the Tom Boy gold mine in southwestern Colorado, in the Savage Basin high above the town of Telluride. How he made it from the docks of New York City to a mining town in the heart of the rugged San Juan Mountains is a lost story, but it must have been an extremely difficult journey.

"I got your grandfather with a box of Sunshine Biscuits," my grandmother said to me with a smile. She went on to explain that the biscuit company's slogan during the war was, "A doughboy in every box!"

—DOROTHY L. CARLSON

Opposite, left: Granddad as a young paperboy in Denver. He delivered papers to the famous "Unsinkable Molly Brown."

Opposite, right: My grandparents, George and Dorothy Carlson, with me, in 1970. I had just graduated from Colorado Academy (high school) in Denver.

Hard-rock mining in Colorado during the 1880s was the most backbreaking and dangerous work imaginable—and all for scant pay. The miners drove the drill steel with sledge hammers and then packed the holes with dynamite. After they tied the pattern of holes together, they cleared the mine and lit the fuse. The mine would shudder from the deafening percussion of the blast, and the dust would drive down the tunnel and burst out of the portal into daylight. While the mine was still full of dust and dynamite fumes, they went back in and began shoveling the broken rock into the ore cars. Their lives were nothing but long, long days of *drill, blast, and muck . . . drill, blast, and muck*. A mine was a smorgasbord of death: Rocks would fall from the ceiling and burst from internal pressure within the walls, timbers might give way, dynamite could explode if mishandled, and on and on. And there was my great-grandfather, only nineteen or twenty years old, alone in a strange land, and learning English on the fly.

Johann eventually made his way to Denver, the thriving capital of Colorado at the eastern edge of the Rocky Mountains on the Great Plains. In a little more than twenty years, Denver had grown from a small frontier town just before the Civil War into a thriving commercial center, with its roots in mining, cattle, and agriculture. On the north side of town were two enormous ore-refining smelters, the Grant and the Argo, whose towering smoke stacks reached into the sky. The city was also a major railhead for shipping cattle to the beef-hungry cities in the East. It was here that Johann made his home. Within Denver's Swedish community, he met his future bride, Amanda Marie Nilsdotter. She was also born in Sweden and came to Denver some time during the late 1880s. They were married and, on July 15, 1894, had their first child, George A. Carlson.

Johann built a contract hauling business and raised Percheron draft horses to pull his ore wagons from the mountain mines to the Grant and Argo smelters. He also did contract hauling for the Lindquist Cracker Company. He and Amanda lived in north Denver on Walnut Street, just a few blocks north of where the sister of William F. Cody (Buffalo Bill) lived. Occasionally, Buffalo Bill would come to Denver for the winter and stay with his sister. As a young boy, Granddad said he and his pals would see the great showman go by in a horse-drawn buggy.

Often, some of Buffalo Bill's employees from the Wild West Show wintered in Denver, doing odd jobs until the traveling show resumed in the spring. Around 1906, when Granddad was twelve years old, one of the Wild West Show workers was hired as a teamster for the Lindquist Cracker Company. Because Johann knew the Lindquists and supplied draft teams for their wagons, young George would help with deliveries on Saturdays. One such

Saturday morning, George went with the Wild West driver to help unload cracker boxes at restaurants and stores in downtown Denver.

As the wagon bumped along down 16th Street, the teamster shouted above the clippity-clop of the horses' hooves, "Son, you're about to meet Buffalo Bill," as he pulled back on the reins of the two-horse team. "Whoa there," he shouted at the huge, plodding drafthorses, as he pulled their chins closer to their chests. As the freight wagon came to a stop alongside the *Denver Post* building, the teamster pulled back on the brake arm. Walking along the sidewalk toward the wagon with his white goatee, wide-brimmed Western hat, and flowing hair was William F. Cody himself. The driver tied off the reins and jumped down and, as he walked in front of the team, shouted back toward the wagon, "Hop on down here, George. Yep, you'll never forget the day you met Buffalo Bill!"

While the driver and the dapper Bill Cody greeted each other and small talk ensued, young George stood by and waited for his chance to meet the great man. Finally, the driver put his arm on George's shoulder and said, "Bill, I want you to meet my helper, George," and they shook hands. Granddad's eyes gleamed with excitement when he told that story, one of the most treasured moments in his long life of eighty-nine years.

As a young boy, Granddad also knew the colorful Molly Brown, famous for surviving the demise of the *Titanic*, for which she became known as "the Unsinkable Molly Brown." This is how he told the story: "One of my first jobs was being a paperboy, and I delivered her paper. One day, she asked me if I could work in her garden during my spare time. So I started taking care of her garden. That was the first job I had working with the earth, flowers, shrubbery, and trees, and, when I was in my late teens, I worked in the greenhouse at the Park Hill Floral Company. Then, before the war, I got a job working for S. R. DeBoer. He was Denver's premier landscape architect, a Dutchman, who came here to design and build the parks and parkways. After the war, I worked for DeBoer again for many years, and we became very good friends." During the late 1950s, Granddad became superintendent of Denver Parks. Although I never heard him say it, I believe his career in landscape architecture and horticulture began by taking care of Molly Brown's garden.

Granddad first showed me the German Luger when I was a young boy. I was sitting on the couch in my grandparent's living room when he went to get the gun in the garage where he kept it hidden. He returned with it resting in his large hands and told the following story: "During the war, when I was alone in the forest of 'no man's land' looking for wounded Americans, a German soldier came out of a thick stand of trees with his hands held above his head, walking toward me." [5] Granddad looked at the pistol and then to me, saying, "The soldier walked slowly up to me and surrendered, offering me his Luger. I was afraid when I saw him and was on my guard, but somehow I knew he meant me no harm. I motioned for him to get in front of me before we started the walk back to the American lines and my company's camp. For that German soldier, the war was over."

After finishing the story, Granddad stepped closer to let me hold the Luger. I extended my small hands, and he placed the gun in my open palms. As I cradled it, I tried to visualize the long-ago scene. Even now, forty-five years later, the image is still powerful in my mind. I can see my grandfather as a young man standing alone in the forest with a German soldier, who had had enough war and just wanted to surrender.

World War I was such a powerful part of my grandfather's life. I can even remember my grandmother, Dorothy, saying with a smile, "I got your grandfather with a box of Sunshine Biscuits." She explained that the biscuit company's slogan during the war was, "A doughboy in every box!" The term "doughboy," which was the name given to the American World War I soldiers, has its roots in the Punitive Expedition of 1916. This military effort was commanded by General John J. Pershing, in which he attempted to capture the infamous Pancho Villa in northern Mexico. As the infantry marched through the alkaline deserts, they were covered in white dust and looked as though they had been rolled in flour. Thus, were called doughboys.

Granddad made sure that his grandchildren had an appreciation for the sacrifices his generation had endured. He often took my brother, Bruce, and me to the Veterans Day parades in downtown Denver. I remember sitting on the curb, watching the military bands, soldiers, and veterans in uniform march proudly by. After the parade, Granddad would take us to Solomon's, an old saloon on Larimer Street. We would sit in a high-backed wooden booth, stained dark with age. The three of us would each have an enormously thick roast beef on pumpernickel sandwich, with a dill pickle and a strawberry pop. Then we would walk down to the south end of Larimer Street where Granddad would let us climb on a replica of the Liberty Bell. Near this corner was the Cootie Club, which, to young boys, sounded terribly funny. But, as he explained to us, *cooties* were what they called the lice that infested their clothing and bedding during the war, and the Cootie Club was an organization of World War I veterans. Every time I drive by that part of town and see that old building, I think of my grandfather.

Granddad was twenty-three years old when he left Denver's Union Station on a "special" train carrying new doughboys to basic training on March 30, 1918. This is where his diary (which he gave the matter-of-fact title, "My Life in the Army") begins. The train was bound for Camp Funston, which was within the Fort Riley military reservation, in the heart of Kansas.

He said goodbye to his friends on the rail platform amid many similar goodbyes happening all around them. Granddad told me his girlfriend was there, but I have forgotten her name. She worked with his sister, Ann, at Joslin's department store. As the eastbound train reached a full head of steam out on the Colorado plains, Granddad had the blues. He had just left those who loved him the most, and he also knew, as did all the other young soldiers in the car, that the conflict in Europe was already the most devastating killing machine in history. The war to stop Kaiser Wilhelm II of Germany from dominating Europe had been raging for more than three years, and millions of young men had died. I picture a thick plume of black smoke drifting over the lonely prairie, as the locomotive pulled the young men off to war.

During basic training, he was assigned to the 353rd Infantry Regiment of the 89th Division, both of which he was reverently proud. This division was known as the Rolling W, which had a symbol with a capital W inside a circle or wheel. The 89th Division was made up of men from the "Middle West," specifically the states of Arizona, Colorado, Kansas, Missouri, Nebraska, New Mexico, and South Dakota.[6] As the symbol is rotated, it changes from M to W (Middle West).[7] The 353rd Infantry Regiment was known as the Kansas Regiment. Their slogan was "We're from Kansas," and their emblem was a sunflower.

Every time Granddad wore a coat and tie after the war, he proudly displayed his Rolling W Pin in his lapel. It measured a half-inch in diameter and was made of brass. The Rolling W of the 89th Division was part of the family lore that my two brothers, my sister, and I grew up with. Granddad faithfully attended their annual reunions in Hutchinson, Kansas, until there were too few veterans to hold a meeting. The 89th Division was Granddad's fraternity, and he was devoted to his brothers in arms throughout his life. They had all helped each other through one of the worst experiences in human history, as well as in their own lives, and they remained loyal to each other, the division, and the American flag. Granddad is buried at the Fort Logan National Cemetery in Denver, surrounded by his fellow soldiers from both world wars. They are in the very best of company.

My siblings and I always knew that he had kept a diary during the war, but I did not see the diary until I was in high school. My mother kept the diary in a desk in the den, and I remember taking it out of the top drawer one evening and just holding it. I looked at a few pages and knew it was something special. I read several passages before putting it back in the drawer, not realizing one day it would become my life's passion. The next time I saw the diary was after Granddad's death in 1983, when my mother gave it to me, along with his 89th Division book. At that time in my life, my wife, Annie, and I were busy raising our two daughters, Lindsay and Cecily, so I put the diary in our safe, again without reading it.

After a few years, I took the diary out and began to read through it. It was a portal into another world. These were not just words on a page; as I read the lines, I could hear Granddad's voice, as if he were right beside me, telling me his story. I transcribed the diary, bought a map of Europe, and began to plot his course. It was exciting and challenging. He traveled through some fifty towns, all of which he spelled phonetically (this made sense, as the names would have been passed down through the ranks by word of mouth). But, in order to track the line-of-march, I needed the French spelling of the towns. So I turned to the maps in the 89th Division Book, which became the key to piecing everything together. Soon I had a feel for the general direction in which the division was traveling at any given time, and it became easier to identify the towns. After many hours of studying the diary and the 89th Division Book, I was able to pinpoint towns and battlefields with some degree of certainty, and thus developed a map of his path through France, Belgium, Luxembourg, and Germany. Before long, I was reading everything I could about World War I—I was hooked and had to go to Europe!

The small, black notebook that Granddad filled with stories of his war travels can fit into a shirt pocket. This little diary has dramatically changed my life. The amazing people I have met, the lasting friendships, the adventurous trips, the life-expanding experiences, and the knowledge I have gained all spring from this tiny book. Now I can share the bounty of my experiences through my own writing and photography. I have reproduced Granddad's entire diary in this book, and the entries are presented exactly as he wrote them. I have used bracketed sections only to clarify word meanings and the correct spelling of the towns. Between the diary, Regimental Book, and 89th Division Book's detailed maps and documentation of troop movement, I know where he was almost on a daily basis for the eleven months he spent in Europe. His journey weaves its way through much of America's involvement in the Great War's complex, sweeping history, and mine illuminates several of America's World War I military cemeteries, monuments, and battlefields.

At age sixty-one, I look back and know that my adventure began with the recollection of Granddad's childhood stories. By walking in his footsteps and imagining his travails and hardships, I discovered how my grandfather's life gave meaning and guidance to my own. I've discovered the history, towns, battlefields, cemeteries, and monuments that figured so prominently in his experience of the war. But more important were the lessons I learned about my grandfather and his courage, his compassion for his fellow soldiers, and the events that shaped his later life.

Though my journey has been full of significant realizations and awakenings, there's one that I consider my moment of commitment. On the morning of November 10, 2005, on the eve of the anniversary of the Armistice, I stood among the white crosses and Stars of David in the American Meuse-Argonne Cemetery in northeastern France, as the ground-hugging mist began to lift. That same mist blanketed those hills eighty-seven years earlier on November 10 and 11, 1918. Looking around me, I felt the presence of the brave, young Americans who were buried there so long ago. Born with freedom imprinted in their hearts, they came from farms, towns, and cities all across the United States to answer their country's call to arms. They came with inexhaustible energy, high ideals, and the determination to put an end to the most destructive and deadly war the world had ever seen. They left their homes, families, and friends to stop a brutal tyranny far from our shores that threatened to dominate Europe and extinguish the flame of freedom. Their lives were cut short, snuffed out in the prime of youth. Never would they experience the joys of marriage, parenthood, grandparenthood, life-long friendships, or any of the millions of experiences that make up a full life. Each made the sacrifice not for his country's conquest of foreign lands, but rather to protect and perpetuate an idea and a sacred way of life—democratic freedom.

Standing among the headstones, I was in awe of their sacrifice and selfless gifts to humankind. It was painful to grasp that the memory of their valorous and courageous deeds were being forgotten. I felt the immensity of the project I was being handed: by following Granddad's war experience, I was also following the path of countless other doughboys. I felt the strength of all those heroes around me, and was moved to make the following vow: "I will do everything I can to keep your memory alive." This book is the realization of that promise, my tribute not only to my grandfather, but to all of America's World War I veterans.

This memorial to the 89th Division in Pueblo, Colorado, was dedicated in March 6, 1927.

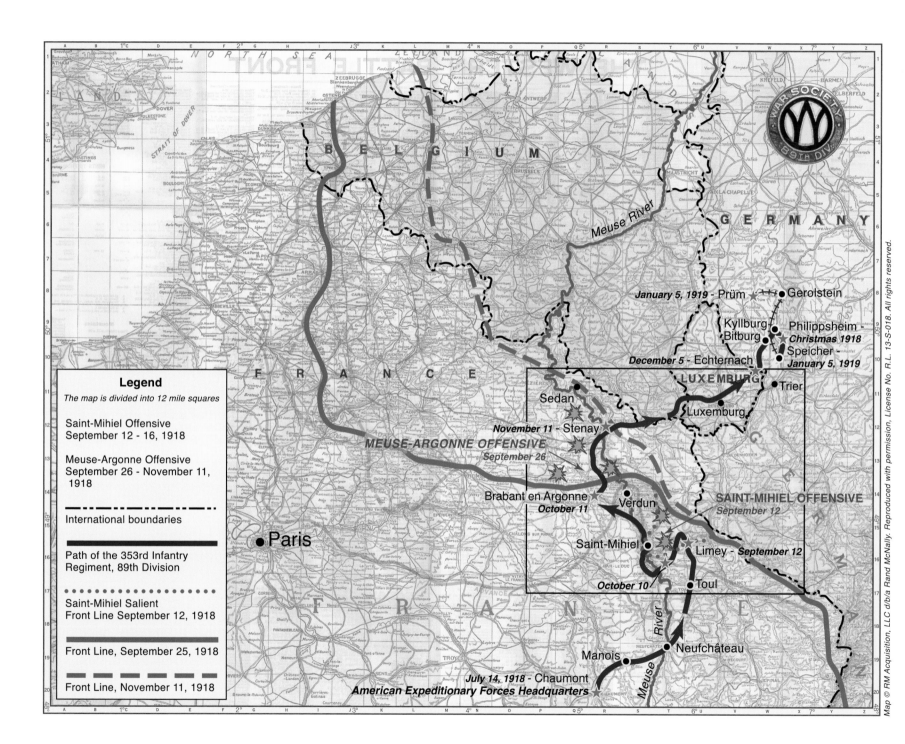

Legend

The map is divided into 12 mile squares

Saint-Mihiel Offensive
September 12 - 16, 1918

Meuse-Argonne Offensive
September 26 - November 11, 1918

— ·· — ·· —
International boundaries

▬▬▬▬▬
Path of the 353rd Infantry Regiment, 89th Division

•••••••••••••
Saint-Mihiel Salient
Front Line September 12, 1918

▬▬▬▬▬
Front Line, September 25, 1918

– – – – –
Front Line, November 11, 1918

NORTH SEA

BELGIUM

GERMANY

FRANCE

Meuse River

LUXEMBURG

January 5, 1919 - Prüm ✪ ⚔ ● Gerolstein

Kyllburg
Bitburg ● Philippsheim - *Christmas 1918*

December 5 - Echternach Speicher - *January 5, 1919*

● Trier

Luxemburg ●

Sedan ●

November 11 - Stenay

MEUSE-ARGONNE OFFENSIVE
September 26

Brabant en Argonne ★ Verdun ●
October 11

SAINT-MIHIEL OFFENSIVE
September 12

Saint-Mihiel ● Limey - *September 12*

October 10 Toul ●

● Paris

Manois ● Neufchâteau ●

Meuse River

July 14, 1918 - Chaumont
American Expeditionary Forces Headquarters ★

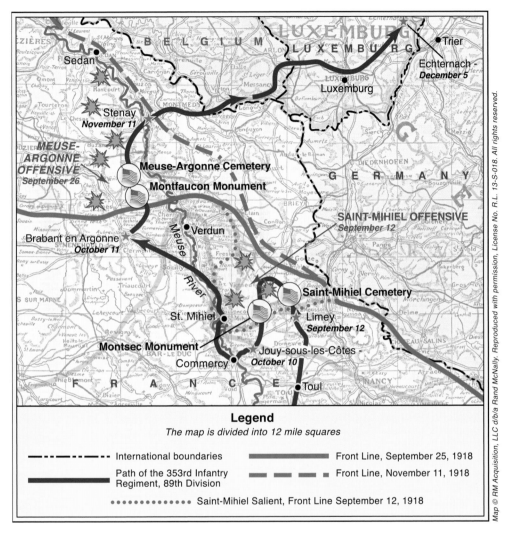

The following text appears on the map:

Sedan

Stenay
November 11

MEUSE-
ARGONNE
OFFENSIVE
September 26

Meuse-Argonne Cemetery

Montfaucon Monument

Verdun

Brabant en Argonne
October 11

Meuse River

BELGIUM

LUXEMBURG

Trier

Echternach -
December 5

Luxemburg

GERMANY

SAINT-MIHIEL OFFENSIVE
September 12

Saint-Mihiel Cemetery

St. Mihiel

Limey
September 12

Montsec Monument

Commercy

Jouy-sous-les-Côtes -
October 10

Toul

FRANCE

Legend
The map is divided into 12 mile squares

— · — · — · — International boundaries

—————— Path of the 353rd Infantry
Regiment, 89th Division

●●●●●●●●●● Saint-Mihiel Salient, Front Line September 12, 1918

—————— Front Line, September 25, 1918

– – – – – Front Line, November 11, 1918

Enlargement of the area indicated on the map opposite.

This map and the one opposite are provided to orient the reader to my grandfather's journey. They have been adapted from a map made by Rand McNally in 1918, which is used by permission. As much as possible and at its request, we have retained the details from the original map; hence the spelling of "Luxemburg" in the map above "North" is understood to be at the top of both maps.

Timeline of Key Events

1914

JUNE 28
Archduke Franz Ferdinand assassinated
in Sarajevo, Bosnia

SEPTEMBER 5–12
French army halts German advance at the Marne River
northeast of Paris, France

MID-SEPTEMBER
German army attacks twenty miles south of Verdun, France,
and advances deep into French territory, forming the
Saint-Mihiel Salient

1916

FEBRUARY 21
Battle of Verdun begins

DECEMBER 18
Battle of Verdun ends

1917

JANUARY 16
British intercepts Zimmermann Telegram

JANUARY 31
Germany initiates unrestricted
submarine warfare

FEBRUARY 3
U.S. severes diplomatic ties with Germany

FEBRUARY 27
President Wilson verifies the Zimmermann Telegram

APRIL 6
U.S. declares war on Germany

JUNE
General Pershing reaches France

1918

MARCH 30
Granddad departs Denver, Colorado,
for Camp Funston, Kansas

MAY 25
89th Division departs Camp Funston
for Camp Mills, New York

JUNE 21
353rd Infantry Regiment arrives in Le Havre, France

JUNE 24

The 353rd Infantry Regiment arrives in Manois, France

JULY 14
Granddad parades at General Pershing's headquarters

AUGUST 3
353rd Infantry Regiment leaves Manois for the front

SEPTEMBER 12
Saint-Mihiel Offensive begins

SEPTEMBER 16
Saint-Mihiel Offensive ends

SEPTEMBER 26
Meuse-Argonne Offensive begins

OCTOBER 10
Granddad arrives in the Meuse-Argonne

LATE OCTOBER
U.S. Army is stalled

NOVEMBER 1
American offensive is renewed

NOVEMBER 11
Armistice is signed, Granddad and Company A
enter Stenay, France

NOVEMBER 24
353rd Infantry Regiment leaves Stenay for Germany

DECEMBER 6
353rd Infantry Regiment crosses the bridge at Echternach,
Luxembourg, and marches into Germany

CHRISTMAS
Granddad is in Philippsheim, Germany

1919

JANUARY 5
Granddad arrives in Prüm, Germany

APRIL 23
Pershing makes final inspection of 89th
Division in Trier, Germany

MAY 7
Granddad and Company A board the train for
the port at Brest, France

MAY 14
From Brest, Granddad and Company A are
homeward bound and set sail for New York City
on the U.S.S. *Leviathan.*

JUNE 28
Treaty of Versailles is signed, officially
ending the Great War exactly five years after
the assassination of the Archduke

The Meuse-Argonne Cemetery in Romagne-sous-Montfaucon, France. There are 14,246 graves and 954 names on the Wall of the Missing at the Meuse-Argonne Cemetery in Romagne-sous-Montfacon, France, which is managed by the American Battle Monuments Commission. The Meuse-Argonne Offensive occurred between September 26 and November 11, 1918.

"The United States did not win the war, but without their economic aid to ease the strain, without the arrival of their troops to turn the numerical balance, and, above all, without the moral tonic which their coming gave, victory would have been impossible."[8]

– British historian Captain Basil Liddell Hart

"Got up and stood revely [reveille] at 6. Gee but this was hard to take."

—GEORGE A. CARLSON, BASIC TRAINING, APRIL 1, 1918

SINCE THE BEGINNING OF THE WAR IN AUGUST 1914, President Woodrow Wilson of the United States had taken a position of neutrality. On January 31, 1917, however, the situation abruptly changed. The German Navy had unleashed a program of unrestricted submarine warfare (the indiscriminant sinking of neutral and Allied ships wherever found). The effect this action had on bringing the United States into the war cannot be overstated. President Wilson immediately broke diplomatic relations with Germany, the first official step toward entry into the war. Then the last straw came in a message of German deceit and treachery—the Zimmermann Telegram from the German Foreign Secretary, Arthur Zimmermann, to the Mexican Consulate in Washington, DC. The White House verified the message on Tuesday, February 27. The telegram attempted to entice Mexico and Japan into declaring war on the United States, so that America would be unable to join the Allies (France and Great Britain) in Europe. In one passage of the telegram, Germany promised funding and military support for Mexico "to regain by conquest her lost territory of Texas, Arizona and New Mexico."[9] Regarding President Wilson's position, historian Barbara Tuchman wrote, "The [Zimmermann] telegram was not the only factor upon the President. It was, rather, the last drop that emptied his cup of neutrality."[10]

On the evening of April 2, 1917, President Wilson addressed a joint session of Congress, including the Supreme Court justices, with a passionate speech explaining the reasons why America should go to war. "[America must] exert all its power and employ all its resources to bring the Government of the German Empire to terms and end the war." His declaration of war continued: "The United States must fight for the ultimate peace of the world and liberation of its people. . . . The world must be made safe for democracy."[11] Thus, on April 6, 1917, the United States entered the war on the side of the Allies by declaring war on Germany.

The senior general, Fredrick Funston, had died of a heart attack in February.[12] Next in line was General John J. "Black Jack" Pershing, who was chosen to command the American Expeditionary Forces in Europe.[13] At the time, the U.S. Army was then only a small peacetime force of 5,791 officers, 121,797 enlisted men, 66,594 National Guardsmen under federal control, and 101,174 National Guardsmen under state control.[14] America was woefully unprepared for a war in Europe. The only battle-ready American troops were 15,000 of the Marine Corps. A conscription system was quickly developed, and 2,810,000 of the most eligible "young and unmarried males without dependents" were called into service.[15] My grandfather was one of those draftees.

Granddad used to say that he "saw Europe on the Uncle Sam plan." His journey began in Denver, Colorado, when Granddad was twenty-three years old.

Mar. 30th, 1918: *Left Denver on a special train for Camp Funston, 9 p.m. Many of my friends were there to see me off. Had a nice time on train, after all the blues had passed.*

Mar. 31st: *Arrived in Camp at 2:30 p.m. Went to a barracks where we waited till we got our first shot, got it about 1 a.m. The first of April I got to (near by) Camp Wood about 4:30 a.m. the same morning. Got up and stood revely at 6. Gee but this was hard to take.*

Apr. 24th: *At 5 p.m. left Camp Wood for Funston arrived about 6:30 p.m. and was sent to "A" Company of the 353 Inf. Reg. 26 of us from the 17 Co.[16] several from Colo. I knew none at that time.[17]*

Major General Leonard Wood commanded the training program of the 89th Division at Camp Funston. He was known as one of the finest training officers in the army. In France, the 89th Division earned an outstanding combat record, which, in large part, was attributed to General Wood.

May 25th 11 a.m.: *Left Funston for Camp Mills. Poor feed on the train. Paraded in K.C., [Kansas City] Mo., Saint Lewis [Louis], got off train and went into the depot and bought some fruit. Paraded in Cleveland, Ohio and Frankford, Ind., went thru Frankford, and Scranton, Pa., paraded in Buffalo, N.Y. arrived in New York City about noon.*

With basic training over, the 89th Division headed to Camp Mills on the Hempstead Plains near Garden City, on Long Island, New York. Along the way, they paraded in Eastern cities to whip up excitement so the public would buy war bonds.

May 28th: *Three days on the road corn beef and hard tack to eat. Took a ferry to Long Island, took train to Camp Mills arrived there 5 o'clock, May 28th.*

May 30th: *I went alone to New York City, and before I knew anything I was walking on fifth Ave, took a ride out fifth Ave in a jitney buss then came back and went to a dance at the Grand Central Palace, got back to Camp about four the next Morning, went to East New York the next night.*

June 3rd: *Left Camp Mills 9 a.m. for the loading docks at Brooklyn where we got on to a small transport. Called the Karanala a British freighter used to make trips to India from England. This was a hell of a boat to be on the deep blue with.*

June 4th, 1 p.m.: *We were turned out for France I was on guard at the time the first time I was on guard in the Army. Everyone was kept down out of sight till we were well out at sea, when we came up we could just see N.Y. and Miss Liberty. At 7:30 p.m. the same day we got a good scare as there were [German] sub-marines in this zone the day before. We were well protected.*

For maximum protection from German U-boats, the U.S. Navy camouflaged the troopships and ran them in a zigzag pattern. Naval destroyers also escorted the convoys.

June 15th, 7 p.m.: *Pulled in to Liverpool, Eng. Layed [in] the harbor all that night and was inspected the next morning and taken off the boat. Marched to a depot where we took a train for a Rest Camp at Manchester had a hard hike to the camp out side of the City four miles. Got there about 2 a.m.*

June 17th: *Sleeping in tents for a couple days, cold and dreary.*

June 21st: *Left for South Hampton where we embarked for France on a sub chaser gee but she was a fast boat. This trip across the English Channel to La Harve [Le Havre] is one trip I never will forget. I feed [fed] the fish about six times it was on a Saturday night to, it was sure a cold trip, made at night.*

Arrival in France and Preparations for War

June 22nd: *Arrived at La Harve, France got off the boat about noon and went to a rest camp a short ways out of town but it was up hill some hike.*

June 23rd, 7 p.m.: *Left La Harve on a freight train, 38 men in a small car like they are all over here.*

By the time the 89th Division arrived, more than 300,000 American soldiers were already in France, many of whom already had experienced the sting of combat. All the while, doughboys were arriving at a rate of 9,000 per day.[18] From the port of Le Havre, on the English channel, Granddad and his regiment went by train to Manois, which is about twenty kilometers (twelve miles) northeast of Chaumont. The freight trains were actually made up of small French boxcars marked *Hommes 40, Chevaux 8*, meaning that they could either carry forty men or eight horses.

June 24th, 8 p.m.: *Arrived at Manois, France a small camp and a small berg only room for four companies, here we started training and believe me we got some training.*

It was in Chaumont where General Pershing, the commander of the American Expeditionary Forces, mindfully set up his headquarters, because it was relatively close to the front and far from the temptations of Paris. Many of the fresh divisions trained in the Chaumont area.

July 4th: *We had a small celebration. I was a K.P. ("kitchen patrol") this day, so I didn't take part.*

Granddad was in Chaumont for only one day, but what a day it was—July 14, Bastille Day! He and his battalion "passed in review" or paraded in front of the legendary general. What a thrilling moment it must have been for him to march past General Pershing, to turn his head toward him and smartly salute the Commander-in-Chief.

This World War I Memorial Statue in Chaumont, France, represents the allegorical mother of France, with her left arm around a poilu, or French soldier, while thanking a doughboy. Chaumont was where the headquarters of General John J. Pershing's American Expeditionary Forces was located.

July 13th, 14th: *Marched 20 kilometers to General Pershing's headquarters [Chaumont] to parade on the 14th of July, France's Liberty Day. We passed in review and then had something to eat, but I made friends with a mail clerk and he had to have me eat with him and I am here to tell you I had some big dinner the best I had had in the Army, this being Mama's birthday, it was some celebration.*

July 15th: *My birthday [the next day] was put in on the road back to Camp, not so good.*

Moving to the Saint-Mihiel Salient

Germany had feared a two-front war since the signing of the 1892 alliance between France and Russia, so the German military developed a plan. Count Alfred von Schlieffen, who was Chief of General Staff of the German military from 1891 to 1906, devised the original strategy, which would become the Schlieffen Plan. The cornerstone of the plan was to advance swiftly into France through neutral Belgium and Luxembourg, the easiest route, and then turn the massive attack south toward Paris before France had adequate time to mobilize. Germany estimated that it could subdue France within six to seven weeks, at which point the German forces could turn eastward and deal with Russia. During the first week of August, before his troops began their march into Luxembourg and Belgium, the Kaiser told them, "You will be home before the leaves have fallen from the trees."[19] It is true that the German Army did return home as the autumn leaves were falling, but not until late November of 1918, after Germany had suffered a staggering defeat and losses of more than 2,000,000 men.

The German Army did indeed sweep across northeastern France and was swiftly marching toward Paris when in early September 1914, the French army finally stopped the Germans at the Marne River some sixty-four kilometers (forty miles) north of Paris. The battle became known as the Miracle on the Marne. In Western Europe, this signaled the advent of trench warfare, which would not allow sweeping advances and swift victories. The grinding war of attrition had begun. The Schlieffen Plan had failed, and the war was in stalemate, but the killing went on and on. Some three and a half years later, this whole progression would lead to battles of immense importance for the American Army and my grandfather.

In accordance with the Schlieffen Plan, during mid-September 1914, the German Army launched a westward attack some twenty kilometers (twelve miles) south of Verdun, France, in an attempt to drive toward Paris. The German juggernaut rolled through the French countryside and left devastation in its wake, but by late September, the French had halted the attack just west of the town of Saint-Mihiel on the River Meuse.[20] The German drive penetrated twenty-six kilometers (sixteen miles) into France from the front line and captured a 200-square miles (320-square kilometers) wedge of territory (or bulge in the front lines) known as the Saint-Mihiel salient. The salient was a threat, "a dagger pointed at the heart of France."[21] The Germans controlled the salient until a U.S. Army attack drove them out exactly four years later with the Saint-Mihiel Offensive of September 12–16, 1918.

Reducing the Saint-Mihiel salient had early on been one of General Pershing's strategic priorities. In order to take on an operation of this magnitude, however, Pershing had to wait until there was a sufficient build-up of American troops. This did not happen until August 1918, when the American forces had swelled to more than 1,300,000 men, with 10,000 more pouring into France daily.[22] So, in early August, General Pershing gathered the numerous divisions (each comprised of 26,000 men divided into four infantry regiments) that had trained in the Chaumont area and began moving them northward to the Saint-Mihiel salient. Ever since General Pershing had arrived in France, the French and British had demanded that American troops be dispersed among their own depleted ranks, but Pershing was adamant that his divisions would fight as an American army. To realize this objective, General Pershing formed the United States First Army on August 10 for the sole purpose of attacking the salient.[23]

By the time he went into battle, Pershing commanded a total troop strength of 550,000 Americans (eighteen divisions) and 110,000 French troops.[24] The First Army's eighteen divisions were divided into the First, Fourth, and Fifth Corps. The First and Fourth Corps were to attack the salient from the southeastern flank and the Fifth from the northwest, while the French would attack the western nose. The 89th Division was part of the Fourth Corps, along with the 2nd and 42nd Divisions.

Aug. 3rd: *Left for the front and was detailed with the supply Co so I went to the front in a wagon train, the rest of the Company went in trucks. I had a nice trip. All night work.*

Aug. 14th: *We went to a place where we got deloused and got some new clothes and a good bath.*

Aug. 22nd: *Went to relieve the second Battalion in the support. We had good dugouts here and also pretty good ones in the front lines. Was only there a few days till we were relived by the third Battalion and we went back to some woods about a kilo. Stayed here till Sept 2nd.*

Sept. 2nd: *We moved up to our old position in the front lines and had a lot of gas and high explosive[s] this time.*

Sept. 4th: *Moved about one kilo to the left, to a big dugout back of the ruined town by the name of Limey, the whole third platoon in one dugout it was sure one big jam, I am here to tell you. A couple of nights later the Germans put over a box barrage on the 353 and the 354 Inf. and made a raid on us, and as a result eight Boshes [Germans] got killed and eight or nine more got wounded.*

THE SAINT-MIHIEL OFFENSIVE (SEPTEMBER 12–16, 1918)

"This was our first full dress Ball."

—GEORGE A. CARLSON, SEPTEMBER, 12, 1918

I FUMBLED FOR THE BLARING ALARM CLOCK in my pitch-black hotel room. It was 4:00 a.m. on the morning of September 12, 2008. Still half asleep, I pulled open the shutters and stood gazing out into the dark and the pouring rain. My first thought was, "This is great, it's just like it was ninety years ago." But that quickly changed to, "Oh, my god!" I had planned for this morning for many months. I was going to walk in Granddad's footsteps at exactly the same time of day he had been here on the ninetieth anniversary of the Saint-Mihiel Offensive. With headlights on high and shoulders hunched close to the steering wheel, I stared at the black road through windshield wipers that couldn't keep up. Driving into the tiny village of Limey-Reménauville, I parked next to an old stone barn and turned off the engine. I sat there in the dark listening to the hammering rain. Finally, I said to myself, "Come on, get going, you have Gore-Tex and an umbrella, and no one is shooting at you." Fitting a small American flag into the outer webbing of my backpack, I heaved it on and started out.

Moving along, I thought how Granddad's description of going "over the top" in his September 11–12 diary entry may seem simple, but the reality of those few words boggles the mind. For Granddad and the majority of the American soldiers, this was their first encounter with combat. They were tired, hungry, and soaking wet from the pounding rain. Furthermore, they had spent the entire night listening to the deafening American artillery barrage of more than 1,000,000 shells. Before dawn and under heavy rain, they crawled out of the muddy trenches into the darkness and into the territory of no man's land. Burdened by a backpack, mud-caked boots, and rifles, they ran into deadly German machine-gun fire.

I was walking not only in Granddad's footsteps, but also upon the field of battle where the American military came of age. Nineteen eighteen was the Year of the Americans. The Saint-Mihiel Offensive was not only a critical battle, but also one that marked a historical series of firsts for the United States military. This was the first American tank battle, commanded by the thirty-two-year-old Lieutenant Colonel George S. Patton, Jr.; the first time that American infantry had support from the Army Air Service, commanded by General Billy Mitchell; and the first usage of the terms H-Hour and D-Day to designate the hour

My walk to commemorate the ninetieth anniversary of the Saint-Mihiel Offensive began here,
at the village of Limey-Reménauville, France.

My commemorative walk took me through several small villages. This is the village of Bouillonville, France.

and the day on which an attack or military operation is to occur. So the first D-Day in American military history was September 12, 1918, not June 6, 1944. But the most significant "first" was that it was the first large-scale American military operation of World War I and the first since the American Civil War. General Pershing got his wish to fight as an American army and noted "the exultation in our minds that here, at last, after seventeen months of effort, an American army was fighting under its flag."[25] I love how Granddad poetically calls this all-American effort "our first full dress ball."

By the time I reached what once was the village Reménauville, the rain had stopped. I opened a small iron gate and walked into what I can only describe as a sanctuary. There were sections of stone columns and blocks strewn upon a grassy area next to a chapel. I noticed that the chapel was constructed with stone blocks of different sizes and colors. What happened here exemplifies the horrors of war. In September 1918, as the German Army advanced, this village was utterly obliterated by artillery fire. Looking beyond the gated area, there were only shell craters. The chapel had been built as a memorial with the rubble of the town. At first I felt as though I was trespassing, but then I felt at ease, knowing my grandfather had been near this solemn place and that it had been given back to the French people by the victorious Americans.

I pressed on and walked the back roads through rolling farmland, past World War I German bunkers, through small villages and the larger village of Thiaucourt, and finally to the American Saint-Mihiel Cemetery. Moving slower now, I walked through the cemetery's gates and made my way to the grave of Second Lieutenant John Hunter Wickersham. His headstone is always easy to find, because of the gold-leaf in the engraving, which signifies the Medal of Honor. (He is the only Medal of Honor recipient in the cemetery.) What also made him so meaningful to me is that he had been in the 353rd Infantry Regiment, and the only soldier in the cemetery from Denver, Colorado.[26] While severely wounded at the Ansoncourt Farm, just west of Reménauville, he kept advancing his platoon until he died from loss of blood on the morning of September 12. Did he and Granddad know each other? Maybe, but regardless, he was the closest connection to Granddad I had in that cemetery. So I placed my little American flag at the base of his headstone. The night before his death, Wickersham had written this somber and prophetic poem.

The Raindrops on Your Old Tin Hat[27]

The mist hangs low and quiet on a ragged line of hills,
  There's a whispering of wind across the flat,
You'd be feeling kind of lonesome if it wasn't for one thing—
  The patter of the raindrops on your old tin hat.

An' you can't help a-figuring—sitting there alone—
  About this war and hero stuff and that,
And you wonder if they haven't sort of got things twisted up,
  While the rain keeps up its patter on your old tin hat.

When you step off with the outfit to do your little bit
  You're simply doing what you're s'posed to do—
And you don't take time to figure what you gain or lose—
  It's the spirit of the game that brings you through.

But back at home she's waiting, writing cheerful little notes,
  And every night she offers up a prayer
And just keeps on a-hoping that her soldier boy is safe—
  The Mother of the boy who's over there.

And, fellows, she's the hero of this great, big ugly war,
  And her prayer is on the wind across the flat,
And don't you reckon maybe it's her tears, and not the rain,
  That's keeping up the patter on your old tin hat?

— J. HUNTER WICKERSHAM

The grave of Second Lieutenant
John Hunter Wickersham from
Denver, Colorado.

THE NINETIETH ANNIVERSARY OF THE SAINT-MIHIEL OFFENSIVE

THE VILLAGE OF FLIERY, just a few kilometers west of Limey-Reménauville, had been on the American front line. I arrived there the next morning, September 13, 2008, for the ninetieth anniversary ceremony of the Saint-Mihiel Offensive. Every ten years, the local French municipalities plan, organize, and fund these magnificent ceremonies to commemorate the Americans and their sacrifices during the Great War. The next series, marking the hundredth anniversary, will be held in 2018.

Several hundred people were at the event, including a French military band. It was still raining, and under my umbrella, I was clicking away with my camera. Then, in the center of the crowd, a French fellow began introducing someone. I was not paying much attention until he said the name: Helen Patton. Snapping my head in their direction, I watched a woman in her early forties walk out of the crowd. She stood there in the rain and, in a powerful, beautiful voice, sang *Amazing Grace* a cappella. I vowed to meet her and introduced myself at the *Vin d'honneur*, or the reception.[28] She told me that she was the great general's

Helen Patton and Remi Foch at the ninetieth anniversary of the Saint-Mihiel Offensive in Fliery, France. Remi is the great-grandson of Marshal Ferdinand Foch, who commanded the World War I Allied armies.

granddaughter and lived in Germany with her physician husband and two teenaged sons. Just then, an older gentleman walked across the wet lawn toward Helen. He was tall and balding, with a large, moonshaped face. When he reached her, they embraced, clearly old friends. Helen turned to me and said, "Jeff, I want you to meet my old friend, Remi Foch.[29] My knees went wobbly, as I shook hands with the great-grandson of the legendary French general, Marshal Ferdinand Foch, Remi's great-grandfather, the commander of the Allied armies during World War I, and, essentially, General Pershing's boss! Luckily, a voice inside my head said, "Take a picture!" Helen and I have been friends ever since.

The brave soldiers of the Saint-Mihiel Offensive did not sacrifice in vain, as it was a great American victory. The attacking 550,000 doughboys took the enemy off guard and within four days had liberated 320 square kilometers (200 square miles) of French countryside and handed the German Army a heavy military and psychological defeat. Historian Martin Gilbert notes that the battle, "as a victory…was seen without blemish."[30] In his final report, General Pershing wrote, "No form of propaganda could overcome the depressing effect on the morale of the enemy of this demonstration of our ability to organize a large American force and drive it successfully through his defenses."[31]

I've stood on Montsec Hill many times, gazing over the battlefield at Saint-Mihiel with the Montsec Monument behind me. Once I even brought Granddad's field glasses, the ones he carried in the war. I swept the grand panorama, looking through the old lenses at the serene, rolling landscape, staring at the same ground where Granddad and the U.S. Army experienced the chaos of clashing armies so long ago. This was a moment of deep connection with Granddad and his contribution to the victory. I was proud to look upon the terrain where the American army first came into its own.

During my 2010 trip, I stayed with my friends Patrick and Marie-Jo Simons, who live near the Saint-Mihiel Cemetery. On a Sunday morning, Patrick and I went in search of the Ansoncourt Farm, where Lieutenant Wickersham was killed. After a few wrong turns in the countryside, we finally found it. We caught the family finishing their breakfast. The farmer, a man in his sixties named Olivier Jacquin, took us out into the farmyard. As we walked, he explained that his farm had been in the family for many generations and showed us the spot where Lieutenant Wickersham had died. He then pointed south to the village of Limey-Reménauville, which was down a gentle slope just a few kilometers away. He told us that, in mid-September 1914, his grandmother took her young daughter (Olivier's mother) and walked to the market in Limey-Reménauville. His grandfather stayed at home with the rest of the children. While at market, the German Army swept in and seized the farm. The family was not reunited until the Americans liberated the salient exactly four years later.

Granddad was in the infantry, so I always wonder how he ended up aligning himself with the medical corps. There are so many questions I wish I could ask him. In his diary excerpts, when he says he "had a lot of work to do," he is referring to caring for the wounded and getting them back to the hospital tents. He soon earned the nickname "Doc."

Sept. 11th: *We ate supper out in a trench and the rain was sure coming down this was about six o'clock, then we went up the trench through the town out in front of it where we stayed in the water up to our knees, and the rain coming down. The barrage started at about 1:10 on the morn of Sept 12th. This was kept up till about 5:20 when we went over what is called the top. We had quite a fight for a few minutes, and a number of our boys got hurt and killed. This was the first All American offensive on both sides of the St. Mihiel salient in Lorraine, which formed part of the fighting line in France. 150 square miles of territory recovered and 15,000 prisoners were taken. This was our first full dress Ball or show. It was reported that about 25,000 captives were taken in less than forty-eight hours. Composed both of Germans and Austrians.*

Sept. 15th: *We sure got heavy shelling only got one meal a day and that was at twelve at night.*

The Montsec Monument, Montsec, France, which is managed by the American Battle Monuments
Commission, commemorates the American sacrifice at the Battle of Saint-Mihiel, September 12–16, 1918.
This offensive was the first large-scale attack conducted by the U.S. Army in the war.

Statue of a young American officer, by
Paul H. Manship, at the Saint-Mihiel
Cemetery, Thiaucourt, France (American
Battle Monuments Commission).

Sept. 12th: I sure had lot of work to do trying to get the wounded boys back that night. I got back to Limey where I slept in the old dugout again. And got something to eat and I hadn't had anything to eat for about 18 hours, and I had taken many men back as well as Boshe [German] prisoners. The last trip I took thirteen Boshe and three wounded men back to the first aid station about five miles in the mud and rain. The Boshe did the work. Our boys took the towns named Thiaucourt and Bullinvilles [Bouillonville], and Zamis [Xammes].

Sept. 13th: *Early in the morning I got up and started for the front where the Company was dug in, there I dug in and slept that night. A couple of days later we moved back five hundred yards and dug in again. Here I dug in with Higgins this is where I got my first cooties [lice].*

Columns of the Montsec Monument (American Battle Monuments Commission) are bathed in light from the setting sun, overlooking the Saint-Mihiel battlefield in Montsec, France.

Sept. 15th: *We sure got heavy shelling only got one meal a day and that was at twelve at night … 150 sq miles of French territory recovered, 15,000 guns were taken … It was reported that about 25,000 captives were taken in less than forty-eight hours, composed of both of Germans and Austrians.*

Sept. 19th: *Were relieved and went back off a hill near Bullinville [Bouillonville] where we got a bath and some new clothes.*

At the ninetieth anniversary ceremony of the Saint-Mihiel Offensive, on September 13, 2008, the Montsec Monument was illuminated for the first time.

The cemetery's chapel at Saint-Mihiel Cemetery in Thiaucourt, France, which is managed
by the American Battle Monuments Commission, has two massive, swinging bronze doors.
The doorknob for each is the head of a doughboy.

Sept. 22nd: *We relieved the 356 Inf in front of Benney what is known as the Benney Woods, [Beney-en-Woëvre] this night was sure a busy night for me. I had five cases in the town, one shell did the work. I lost my Co. and with one of the wounded men we started to find the Co. found them in the Woods about twelve o'clock. That night, we were under heavy shell fire all the time. Shell[s] bursting all around us every minute, and awfully dark in fact it had been dark every night for a long time before that night.*

The Saint-Mihiel Offensive battlefield near Nonsard, France.

Oct. 1st: Moved about four Kilos to the left to relieve the 42nd Div. This was another bad place heavy shelling all the time [and] bad water to drink. We had plenty to eat at this place. I had a lot of work doing gas guard and carrying wounded men.

Oct. 9th: *We were relieved by the 37th Div. and we went back four kilos to St. Baniot [St. Benoît-en-Woëvre], where we took trucks and went to a town by the name of Joy [Jouy-sous-les-Côtes] about six hours ride.*

There are 4,153 graves and 284 names on the Wall of the Missing at the Saint-Mihiel Cemetery in Thiaucourt, France. Engraved at the base of the American Eagle is General John J. Pershing's famous quote, "Time will not dim the glory of their deeds."

First Army Moves to the Meuse-Argonne: Accomplishing the Impossible

A run was arranged to commemorate the ninetieth anniversary of General Pershing moving the First Army in order to open the Meuse-Argonne Offensive on September 26. A candle from a Sacred Flame within the chapel at the American Saint-Mihiel Cemetery was used to light the runner's torch. The flame is symbolic of the Sacred Flame that is kept in a memorial tower in the town of Verdun. The Sacred Flame honors the horrendous casualties (approximately 500,000) suffered by the French in 1916 while defending the Verdun area from continual German assaults.[32] It was late afternoon on September 20, 2008, and the French National Police running team would later carry the torch northward some sixty kilometers (thirty-six miles) to the American Montfaucon Monument in the Meuse-Argonne region.

Immediately following the Saint-Mihiel victory on September 16, the exhausted doughboys had to gather their strength and begin moving northward with all of their armaments and supplies to the Meuse-Argonne region, where the offensive was scheduled to begin less than two weeks later. The rain, endless mud, difficult terrain, and overwhelming logistics made the transfer an awesome task. Furthermore, operations had to be carried out at night, without lights, and in complete secrecy from German intelligence—including the construction of aerodromes, rail lines, hospitals, and supply depots. The line of trucks and horse-drawn artillery for a single division stretched for thirty-two kilometers (twenty miles).[33] Though this movement of the troops is rarely given the credit it is due, it was truly one of the most incredible feats that the U.S. Army accomplished during the war and an unparalleled achievement in military history. For an army to win a major battle, then move fifty kilometers (thirty miles) over difficult ground and open an even grander offensive—all within fourteen days—approaches the impossible. The mastermind who planned this unrivaled operation was Colonel George C. Marshall (nicknamed the Wizard), who later served as the Army Chief of Staff during World War II and played a key role in the defeat of Nazi Germany and Imperial Japan.

The 89th Division, along with the 1st, 2nd, and 4th Divisions, stayed behind to secure the salient. Granddad and his regiment made the arduous journey by truck convoy on

Re-enactors of a doughboy and his French equivalent, or poilu, *at Saint-Mihiel Cemetery, during the opening of the torch lighting ceremony.*

October 10. This is the only time he mentions riding in a truck between the period of early August, when they left Chaumont, and mid-December 1918, when they arrived in Prüm, Germany, for the Allied occupation. They walked, mostly in the mud, an estimated 450 kilometers (about 270 miles).

For the ninetieth celebration, the relay team of runners followed the same roads and ran the distance at night, remaining true to history. The runners would stop in every town and village along the way for a ceremony honoring General Pershing, Colonel George C. Marshall, and, of course, the doughboys. Before the head runner, Ludovic Livernais, left the Saint-Mihiel Cemetery, I gave him a small American flag to carry in honor of my grandfather and the doughboys. There was a small parade of support vehicles that trailed Ludovic as he left the cemetery. Two vans carried the alternating runners, the third held a generator as well as the light poles and audio equipment for the ceremonies, and a fourth van con-

Ludovic Livernais, the lead runner, carries the torch, as well as the small American Flag I gave him at the Saint-Mihiel Cemetery before the run began.

veyed the ceremony officials and photographers. But the last in the caravan, which symbolized the commemoration, was an authentic, perfectly restored World War I Ford ambulance that had been loaded on a trailer and pulled by a car.

It was dusk when the runners reached the American Montsec Monument. A podium was set up, the sound speakers put in place, and a woman addressed the crowd in French. During the speech, she would periodically say, "Merci, General Pershing, merci, George Marshall, et merci, doughboys!" It was dark by the time the runners reached the town of Saint-Mihiel, so the light poles went up. This process went on all through the night at every village along the route. By dawn, the runners were within sixteen kilometers (nine miles) of the Montfaucon Monument.

Here a group of ten or so NATO soldiers joined the runners for the final push. They were from all over Europe: Belgium, France, Italy, Poland, and even Germany. My friend Lieutenant Colonel Douglas Mastriano and another officer represented the U.S. Army. [34]

When the runners arrived at the monument, they were met by cheering crowds. Ludovic was the final runner and carried the torch. He ran up the many stairs to the base of the monument, holding the torch high. In the room at the base of the monument, he lit a candle with the torch, and the transfer of the Sacred Flame was complete.

NATO runners participate in the run that commemorated General Pershing's movement of the First Army from the Saint-Mihiel region to the Meuse-Argonne. Lieutenant Colonel Douglas Mastriano is third from the right.

Oct. 10th: *We got new and clean underwear and that afternoon we took trucks, went to the Verdun sector. The Argonne woods are in the Verdun sector. Took about twenty-six hours to ride that distance.*

Oct. 11th: *Hiked to a town about four kilos from where we got off the trucks this town was call [ed] Brabant [en Argonne].*

The Montfaucon Monument in Montfaucon, France, commemorates the American sacrifice at the Meuse-Argonne Offensive. The Ford ambulance was there for the ninetieth anniversary of General Pershing secretly moving the First Army from the Saint-Mihiel Battlefield to the Meuse-Argonne sector in mid-September 1918. The American Battle Monuments Commission manages the monument.

THE MEUSE-ARGONNE OFFENSIVE
(SEPTEMBER 26–NOVEMBER 11, 1918)

"A lot of our boys were wounded in this battle. I am here to tell you it was some battle too, the boys were getting bumped off like flys in the fall."

—GEORGE A. CARLSON, OCT. 22, 1918

ON A WARM JUNE DAY IN 2007, Phil Rivers, then superintendent of the American Meuse-Argonne Cemetery, walked with me along a muddy trail deep in the Argonne forest. He told me, "The Argonne was the hardest nut the Allies had to crack. The German Army had been here for four years building their defenses and they were here to stay. They had endless rows of trenches that were more than thirty-three kilometers (twenty miles) deep. They had two critical reasons to defend the Meuse-Argonne. First, this region protected their vital war supply rail depot at Sedan, and, secondly, if breached, the road to Germany lay open to the Allies. Everyone knew that, if Sedan fell, the game would be over."

We were walking to the spot in the forest where Lieutenant Colonel Douglas Mastriano[35] believes, after thorough research and fieldwork, Sergeant Alvin York captured 132 German prisoners on October 8, 1918. The legends that sprang from the Meuse-Argonne are some of the richest in all of American military history. Two of the most famous stories are those of the Lost Battalion and of Sergeant Alvin York.

On October 2, Major Charles W. Whittlesey, who commanded a battalion from the 77th Division, led a forward mission deep into the Argonne forest. The battalion was comprised of "six companies of 308th Infantry (Regiment) and one (company) of the 307th, together with elements of a machine gun battalion."[36] By that evening, they had reached the foot of a steep-sided ravine that would become known as "the pocket." The Germans, meanwhile, moved troops southward during the night and, by morning, had surrounded the battalion. Whittlesey and his 600 men, hopelessly trapped, were relentlessly mauled by German machine gun and mortar fire. Compounding the disaster, on the second day, American artillery batteries used coordinates that fell short of the enemy line and rained destruction onto the battalion. In a desperate attempt to stop the "friendly fire," the Americans released their last homing pigeon, "Cher Ami," with the message: "Our own artillery is dropping a barrage directly on us. For heaven's sake stop it."[37] Shortly after "Cher Ami" fluttered back to division headquarters, the artillery barrage was stopped. The German commanders offered Whittlesey and his men the chance to surrender, but he declined.

In an effort to rescue the men of the trapped battalion, the 77th Division attacked the Germans from the south, and the 82nd Division followed suit from the northeast, together forcing the Germans to pull back from their positions surrounding "the pocket." Relief finally came when the 307th Infantry (77th Division) punched through to "the pocket" from the south on the evening of October 7.[38] The next day, after five days of unyielding assaults, only 194 of the soldiers under Whittelsey's command, mostly wounded, could walk out. The tragedy would be immortalized as the story of the Lost Battalion.

The 82nd Division was continuing the assault on the Germans on the morning of October 8, when another remarkable event took place in the Argonne Forest. Just west of the village of Châtel-Chéhéry, the attack was stopped by heavy German machine-gun fire. Seventeen men from Company G of the 328th Infantry Regiment, under the command of Sergeant Bernard Early, were sent to outflank the position in an effort to silence the enemy fire. In the process, Early's patrol surprised a small group of German officers having breakfast at their headquarters' camp. The Americans attacked, and the officers began to surrender. As the American patrol was securing the prisoners, enemy fire erupted from a nearby hillside, killing or wounding nine men, including Early.

Phil Rivers, deep in the Argonne Forest.

Meanwhile, Alvin C. York, a backwoodsman and expert marksman from Tennessee, had dropped to the ground when the shooting started. He patiently waited for enemy heads to pop up from their hidden positions, sighted his target, and pulled the trigger, again and again. He never missed. When later asked by Major General George Duncan, commanding officer of the 82nd Division, how many he thought he might have shot, York modestly replied, "General, I would hate to think I missed any of them shots; they were all pretty close range, fifty or sixty yards."[39] After decimating the German gun positions, York organized a column of German prisoners and started back to the American lines. Later that day, the tall, raw-boned York gave his report to the brigade commander, General Lindsay. "Well York, I hear you captured the whole damned German Army!" exclaimed the General. Unassumingly, York replied, "No sir, I only have 132."[40] The record credits York with taking 132 prisoners, killing twenty-five, and silencing thirty-five machine guns. That morning, Alvin C. York walked out of the Argonne forest and into the annals of American military mythology. Both Major Whittlesey and Sergeant York received the Congressional Medal of Honor.

During the small hours of September 26, 1918, the thunderous roar of the American artillery signaled the beginning of the battle. The cannon barrels belched fire into the darkness, as if the gates of hell had been flung open. The battle of the Meuse-Argonne was a kind of Armageddon. In terms of troop numbers it remains "the largest [and] also the deadliest battle in American history."[41] The price of victory was enormous; the U.S. Army suffered more than 100,000 casualties with 26,277 deaths recorded in forty-seven days.

This opening barrage pounded German positions until dawn, when the doughboys went "over the top" and charged into the pages of history. At the battle's end, there were forty-two American divisions totaling 1,250,000 men. As the battle intensified along the twenty-mile front, 10,000 fresh doughboys poured onto the front lines every day. There were also 135,000 French troops, under General Pershing's command.[42] This offensive, which was part of a massive Allied drive all along the western front, helped bring the German Army to collapse. Although it was a Franco-American effort, it was primarily an American offensive, which ended in victory and forced the German Army to sign an armistice, or cease-fire, on November 11, 1918.

The landscape of the Meuse-Argonne region is made up of a series of broad north-south trending, open valleys separated by heavily forested ridgelines and solitary hills. The serene, rolling countryside is majestic in autumn, with soft colors, billowing clouds, and sweeping vistas. While walking the ridgelines on numerous trips there, I've marveled at the thought of how, as the autumn leaves fell in 1918, the landscape became hell on Earth.

For the German Army, the ridgelines offered perfect, natural defensive positions. They had spent the previous four years building seemingly impregnable defensive structures atop these ridgetops, complete with deep, concrete bunkers with electricity, connecting tunnels, trench systems, barbed wire strung endlessly, countless machine gun nests, permanently mounted artillery, tank traps, and railroad lines to supply positions and to rotate troops. For these reasons, the region was a nightmare for the doughboys, who were forced to run unprotected across the open valleys, much like Pickett's Charge at Gettysburg, during the Civil War, where the Southern attackers ran fatefully across a mile-wide field straight into Union guns.

Due to the enormous number of troops, General Pershing relinquished his command of First Army to Lieutenant General Hunter Liggett. Also, before the battle began, the Second Army was formed. Joining the fray, the 89th Division began arriving during the second week of October (Granddad arrived on October 10) and was assigned to the Fifth Corps of the First Army. The Fifth Corps also included the 1st, 2nd, 32nd, and 42nd Divisions.[43]

Throughout early October, General Pershing's troops made significant northward advances against the enemy, but, by the end of October, the U.S. Army had stalled. The brutal effects of non-stop, full-on frontal attack were taking their toll on the American army, as were the fog and rain that beset them throughout the battle. Exhausted from heavy enemy resistance, the Americans desperately needed rest and a more effective combat strategy. Right when they thought the situation could not get any worse, the global influenza epidemic of 1918 struck. During October, 15,000 cases were diagnosed, and it is thought that even Pershing may have contracted the disease.[44] Adding to the problems, the Army Air Service was unable, due to poor weather, to contribute to the battle as it had at Saint-Mihiel. The American army was learning how to fight more effectively under the worst of circumstances.

After finally pausing to regain their strength, the Americans realized that a change in strategy was needed. The traditional tactic of using an artillery bombardment followed by an infantry charge was not working. Major General Edward F. McGlachlin of the 1st Division had the answer. He and his staff perfected the "rolling barrage." It was a simple concept: Keep the concentrated artillery shells pounding just forward of the infantry's advance, thus continually protecting the troops with a wall of fire. It was critical to move the artillery constantly ahead instead of keeping it at the rear, thereby always staying within range. The artillery officers learned to adjust the rolling barrage to match the terrain the infantry was confronting: "One hundred meters every four minutes on open ground, six minutes up slopes, eight through woods."[45]

As the U.S. Army prepared for this second offensive, an astonishing total of 1,867,723 were now on the front lines.[46] In planning the "break out," it was decided that the 2nd and 89th Divisions of Fifth Corps, both of which were positioned in the center of the American line, would be the vanguard of the attack. General Wright of the 89th Division roused his staff: "This can well be the climax of the Division's service. That is what we have been living for. Burn this into your minds. Tell it to your men. Hold them together. Set your teeth."[47]

Thus, the army initiated a new offensive with concentrated artillery power on November 1. The roar of the artillery signaled a newly revitalized American army. The sky was "alight from then until daybreak with the constant flashes seeming to come from every ravine for miles to the rear. The ground shook to the explosions. It was the supreme power of Artillery, absolute devastation."[48] As the 2nd and 89th Divisions advanced, the other divisions pushed ahead on their flanks. Because of improved weather, the Army Air Service also sprang into action and supported the infantry by flying low strafing runs over the enemy. This intense combination of power proved spectacularly successful, as the two divisions sprinted forward over seven kilometers (four miles) on the first day. By the evening of the second day, the German lines had been smashed. The German Army was then in full retreat. With the enemy defenses crumbling, the German command desperately sought a cease-fire. The all-important rail supply depot at Sedan was taken by French troops on November 10, which eliminated the German Army's lifeline. Kaiser Wilhelm's bid to dominate Europe had been crushed.

The armistice was signed in Marshal Foch's private rail coach near the village of Compiègne early on the morning of November 11, 1918. It was to take effect at 11:00 a.m. that day, as the Allied drafters wished to create a numerical alignment (the eleventh month, eleventh day, and eleventh hour) that would have the greatest impact upon the collective memory. The Great War was not officially over, however, until the Treaty of Versailles was signed on June 28, 1919, exactly five years after the death of the Archduke Franz Ferdinand.[49] The war had led to nearly 20,000,000 deaths, half from combat and half from disease and famine.

The Meuse-Argonne Offensive is generally recognized as the defining battle that forced the German Army to capitulate. Even German command stated the "war was lost in the Argonne."[50] Pershing's army had broken through the impenetrable Argonne and opened the door to Germany. The immense American sacrifice during the Meuse-Argonne Offensive helped catapult the United States onto the world stage. When America entered the war in April of 1917, its military was ranked seventeenth in the world; after the Meuse-Argonne Offensive, it was a superpower.

At the 2005 Armistice Day (Veterans Day) commemorative ceremony at the Meuse-Argonne Cemetery, Phil Rivers gave me a nudge and said, "See that older gentleman over there with all the medals on his blazer? He was wounded on D-Day."[51] I walked over and introduced myself. His name was Bill Ryan, a retired command sergeant major. It was the beginning of a good friendship. Ryan had been in the 16th Infantry Regiment of the 1st Division (the Big Red One) and wounded in the first assault wave on Omaha Beach. He said matter-of-factly of D-Day, "I was finally evacuated that evening and taken back to England. Then they patched me up, put me into the 82nd Airborne Division, and sent me into the Battle of Market Garden. So, on September 17, I parachuted into Holland at the Nijmegen Bridge." He went on to fight in the Battle of the Bulge and on through the end of the war. He also served in the Korean and Vietnam wars. Bill is an American hero.

Bill and I intentionally met up again in the Meuse-Argonne on September 26, 2008, for the ninetieth anniversary ceremonies of the great battle, which took place at several villages throughout the day. At one village, we saw a French doughboy re-enactor with an 89th Division Rolling W shoulder patch. We also saw an incredible display given by a fellow who flew a British Sopwith Camel bi-plane from Paris and buzzed the energized crowd.

Every ten years, the local townspeople from surrounding villages produce a magnificent pageant, with a cast of several hundred, at the American Montfaucon Monument to honor the Americans who fought there in World War I. Intended for a French audience, the play portrays the French farmers peacefully working in the fields until German soldiers invade. The French soldiers, the *poilu*, unsuccessfully try to fight the Germans and are taken prisoner. When all looks lost, the doughboys appear to defeat the Germans and give the land back to the villagers.

I arrived early, and Phil Rivers had saved me what he called "the best seat in the house," which turned out to be in the middle of the temporary bleachers on the top row. Including the few American personnel from the Meuse-Argonne cemetery, I was among only a handful of Americans at this event. I set up my tripod and began taking practice shots with my camera. Soon the crowds began to fill the stands. I was sitting there, wearing my American flag cap, when a lady, climbing the steps, stopped and stared at me. With quizzical eyes, she asked in broken English, "Are you an American?" I replied proudly, "Yes, I am!" She then asked, "Why are you here?" I explained that my *grand-père* was a doughboy, and I was here to honor him and all the doughboys. She gazed at me approvingly for another moment and then said, "We are so glad you are here."

On the ninetieth anniversary of the Meuse-Argonne Offensive, Bill Ryan, an American World War II veteran, stands next to a French doughboy re-enactor wearing a 89th Division Rolling W shoulder patch. The ceremony took place in the village of Neuvilly-en-Argonne.

A British Sopwith Camel bi-plane helps commemorate the ninetieth anniversary
of the Meuse-Argonne Offensive.

French re-enactors at the ninetieth anniversary ceremony of the Meuse-Argonne Offensive in the village of Neuvilly-en-Argonne. A French officer is in the foreground, and doughboys are in the background.

French re-enactors at the ninetieth anniversary ceremony of the Meuse-Argonne Offensive in the village of Neuvilly-en-Argonne. To the right is a French army chaplain, and behind him are Red Cross nurses.

Oct. 12th: Moved a little farther back to some big woods where we were supposed to rest but we drilled, and here we were replaced with some men from the 86th Div. And a day later we moved up closer to the front, here we stayed till Oct 19th when we moved up to the Bantheville Woods. This whole system of woods is known as the Argonne Woods. We got to our positions some time after midnight and My Pal Higgins and I didn't dig in we just tied our tent to a couple of trees and went to sleep. We got heavy shelling here. The same morning we got up and dug ourselves a good hole in the ground. Gee as much as it was raining, we were afraid to drink any of it as they had some mustard gas a few day[s] before and it stays in the ground and on the trees. So Hiney and I went to try and find a spring. When we got back it was about nine o'clock and we sure was wet. We didn't get anything to eat but did get some water, but when we got back we tried to get kinda dry, an hour later the order came to move to the rear, so there we were no rest and another hole to dig, nothing to eat.

The western gates of the Meuse-Agronne Cemetery, Romagne-sous-Montfaucon, France.

Oct. 20th: *We moved about eleven, we moved back to what was supposed to be five hundred yards but it was three times that far, here I didn't get to sleep with my pal as I had a heavy load and couldn't make it as fast as the Co. Well this night my Pal got hurt and had I been sleeping with him, I would have got hurt as I always slept on that side of the dugout. There were a lot of boys wounded and killed this night.*

A French World War I cemetery near the village of Vienne-le-Château in the Argonne Forest.

The Meuse-Argonne Cemetery in Romagne-sous-Montfaucon, France, on the morning of November 10, 2005, the eve of the anniversary of Armistice Day.

Oct. 21st: Another fellow and I dug in and that night we were on gas guard again as usual. About eleven that night we got the order to move to the front line and we did. We got there about two the morning of the 22nd had a couple of hours sleep and then we dug a hole for the Co. Commander. About noon we had something to eat.

Oct. 22nd: *We we[re] eating when the order came in to what they call Police-up the woods in front of us, but what I call drive the Dutch [Germans] out of the woods. We moved-up on the Germans and got up to within 40 to fifty feet of them before they knew we were there. You understand the woods were thick. This was a hell of a job as we had no barrage to give us some kind of help. A lot of our boys were wounded in this battle. I am here to tell you it was some battle too, the boys were getting bumped off like flys in the fall. I sure had a lot to do here, it is a wonder that I wasn't killed at this place as the bullets were sure flying high and low, and the boys were falling all around me. I tell you, our company was sure small after this battle.*

The Bantheville Woods, near where Granddad and his company were engaged in combat on October 22, 1918.

Oct. 22nd: *I worked all the rest of that day and that night till I thought I would drop in my tracks. I sure carried a lot of boys that day and night. That is where I got my name, Doc. One of the boys out of the 86 Div. said he never did hear my name before, but when we got in to the battle all he could hear was "first aid and Carlson." And he said every time he looked up he saw me running or fixing up some one, and the next day my old Corp[sman] started to call me Doc Carlson and my name still stays with me. Well I sure did a lot for the boys that day and night when they would be laying behind a tree or in the ground. I would be out in the open helping some of the wounded to the rear or fixing them up and putting them in a safe place. I got back to the first aid station that night about 12 o'clock and the next day I went to the Co again. I had just got there when I had to make a trip back with one of the Officers. That night if it hadn't been that I knew the direction as well I did, I could have went [gone] in to the German lines as we were supposed to have the 354 Inf on our left and when we came to find out they were not there, but got there later. I sure had a hard time getting to the Co. that night, the night of Oct 23rd.*

Oct. 31st: *We moved back to the reserves about five kilos we were to go to our new positions by Platoons. I was to lead the way for the third Platoon to a certain point and from there a fellow from the Co. that relieved us was to take the lead. Well, I got to the place where I was to go but the other fellow lost the whole bunch of us, so it was up to me to get back to where this fellow took charge. I did this and he tried again, but the same thing happened in the mean time we were getting heavy shelling, and I said to one of the Sergeants that if this fellow didn't find out where he was taking us, I would go to a dugout and stay there till the next morning, that I knew where there were a lot of them [dugouts]. About that time about a dozen shells came pretty close to us and the Serg. said "Carlson, where are those dugouts[?"] so I took the whole Co. and put them in those holes. After I had this all done my pal and I went to the kitchen to get some thing to eat as we hadn't [had] any supper. I was the only one who knew where it was, and knew it wasn't far. A couple hours the runner or lead got his mind together and went to the place where we were supposed to go and came back and took us to the position, it was just getting day light and we each got a hole as usual. My Corp[s] found a man's hand in the hole. He [thought] the fellow who had slept there that night got his hand blowed off.*

The Pennsylvania State World War I Monument, in Varennes-en-Argonne, France, honors the Pennsylvania National Guard, 28th Division, which liberated the west side of the town of Varennes on the first day of the Meuse-Argonne Offensive, September 26, 1918.

The Meuse-Argonne Cemetery in
Romagne-sous-Montfaucon, France.
A small percentage of the American
Expeditionary Forces was Jewish.

Nov. 1st: *The barrage started about one o'clock this morning and we knew we were going over [the top] that morning in reserves of the 2nd and 3rd battalions. We were all sleeping when it (The Germans had the Argonne wood trenched back 27 miles.) started, wasn't anything new to us. About daylight the 2nd Battalion went over with the 3rd in support and we went over about 8:30 a.m. in reserves of the 2nd and 3rd Battalions. We advanced about four kilos and stayed in some woods that night of course the 2nd battalion went farther as they were doing the fighting.*

Nov. 2nd: *We followed the boys up some more and stopped for the night in some more woods, but just about the time we got dug in, the order came to move, so we moved about a kilo toward the front, and again dug in. My pal and I and another fellow were digging in together, we got awfully hungry so I was to go up to the road where the shelling was heavyest to see if I couldn't find some bread or canned meat on some of the German prisoners that were going by there. I went through a couple hundred of them and only found a small can of meat. I went back to the boys to eat it and help them dig in. I had just got back when a shell hit pretty close to us and pieces of it came down right between the three of us. We were lucky. I say it could have kill[ed] all three of us had it hit right. We got the hole done and then we put down our Dutch blankets and went to bed.*

The Meuse-Argonne Offensive battlefield near Remonville, France.

Nov. 3rd, 2 A.M.: *The order came for me and my pal who was helping me at this time to go out to where the 2nd Battalion were fighting and aid in helping the wounded men back. It had been raining as usual and was an awful trip but we did it. We got a man and [got] him to the aid station, which at that time was in Remonville. Here we rested up and got something to eat and that afternoon we made for the front again. Got [caught] up to where the Co. was but they had moved farther ahead so we stayed in the hole that we had dug the night before.*

Nov. 4th: *My pal and I got up and rolled up our blankets and started to find the Co. We walk[ed] till late in the afternoon all the time going ahead and we got in to Tialey [Tailly] about an hour ahead of the Co. There we joined them and a couple of the boys said there is Doc & Spencer [and] I am so glad to see them. What if something would happen to us who would take care of us, if they weren't here[?] We stayed near Tialey till about twelve that night when we got orders to move forward. [Walter G. Spencer of Pueblo, Colorado, and Granddad were life-long friends.]*

Nov 5th: *We marched the rest of the night and about daylight stopped in front of Beauclair. Spencer and I layed down on the ground and slept a while an[d] we got so hungry that we got up and went to town to see if we could get something to eat. Gee I never will forget how they were shelling that town, but we went anyhow at the risk of our lives and all we got was a can of tomatoes. I eat half of them and he couldn't eat any so we left them.*

Nov. 9th: *Ordered to move to the front and was on our way when the order came to move back to Tialey so we turned around and went back there. Got there about twelve went to sleep in an old barn.*

The Armistice

"We sure were surprised after eleven o'clock when we could hear no more guns firing."

—George A. Carlson, November 11, 1918

I can still hear Granddad's soothing voice telling his story of the Armistice:

It was the evening of November 10, and our company was camped near the old train station on the west side of the Meuse River. We stayed up all night and talked because we knew in the morning we would all be killed. On the other side of the river was the town of Stenay and our orders were to attack Stenay in the morning. When the Germans retreated they dynamited the bridge, so huge blocks of concrete were scattered in the river. The only way across was to 'pick' our way from block to block and we knew there was a German machine gun in every window of the town pointed at the demolished bridge. But early the next morning a messenger rode through camp and told us that the Armistice had been signed. Later that morning I was the eighth or ninth man across the river and we went into town without a fight. We sure were lucky as most of the Germans had retreated during the night.

As it turned out, Granddad and his company had been extremely fortunate that morning. Stenay was a small window in the front line where the majority of German soldiers had retreated during the previous night. All along the front to the north and south of Stenay, German troops were still in position. On the morning of the 11th, both sides (Allied and German) knew an armistice had been signed. Tragically, however, some ambitious Allied officers pushed an attack that morning right up to the eleventh hour, as they saw an opportunity to advance their careers. One last punch, one last objective, one last promotion. Revenge and a parting chance to punish the Germans were also motives in the deadly finale. The Germans were finished and only fought back in self-defense. As a result, the morning of the Armistice became one of the deadliest days of the war.

The day before Armistice Day (Veterans Day) 2011, I was visiting with David Bedford, the new superintendent of the Meuse-Argonne Cemetery, in his office when he asked me, "How would you like to read the President's annual Veterans Day Proclamation at tomorrow's ceremony?" I looked at him with some surprise, thought for a moment, and then replied, "That would be a great honor for me, but I have a better idea. A friend of mine,

Charlie Slosson, is driving over from Wiesbaden (Germany) tomorrow for the ceremony and he is an army officer. [52] If Charlie agrees, I think he should read the proclamation. I'll give Charlie a call and will let you know." I was staying in Stenay at the home of my friends, David and Marian Howard, so on my way back to town I called Charlie. Before I could finish the question he cried, "I would love to!"

The cold fog hugged the ground, as many in the reverent, silent crowd glanced at their watches. In the waiting, time stood still. Then a lone bell in the chapel tower tolled with a low tone that gently rolled over the graves and spilled out into the countryside. With its slow cadence the bell tolled ten more times. It was the sacred eleventh hour on Armistice Day 2011 at the Meuse-Argonne Cemetery.

After the tone of the final bell, everyone stood there in awe of the meaning of those eleven bells. There was absolute silence. Then Major Charles Slosson began reading the proclamation in a strong and steady voice. He read with the conviction that can only come with historical reverence and knowing that, at that moment, he represented the U.S. Army. It was a moment in my life I will never forget.

Major Charles Slosson (left) reads the President's annual Veterans Day Proclamation at the Meuse-Argonne Cemetery on November 11, 2011. Dominique Didot (middle), representing the American Battle Monuments Commission, serves as the translator. To the far right is a member of the fire department (pompiers) of the village of Romagne.

Nov. 10th: *Left Tialey when [went] through Beauclair and up to the Stenay Depot where there was a large dugout used at one time for a waiting [staging?] room. The whole Co. and a machine gun Co. got into this place. Here we were to stay while they put the barrage over till daylight. And we had several patrols out to see where we could cross the River Meuse and go into Stenay the morning of the 11th.*

Nov. 11th [Armistice Day]: *That morning we received the news that the Armistice was to be signed, and we all kind a raised up with a relief, but sank down and said Bull. It was about five o'clock then all most daylight. And about nine o'clock that morning we went in to Stenay. The third Platoon in which I am in was the first to cross the Meuse River. At that point I was about the eighth or ninth man to cross. Spencer and I took four prisoners and then got in to a French house and had some thing to eat. The French people we[re] sure glad to see us. I am here to tell you.*

We sure were surprised after eleven o'clock when we could hear no more guns firing.

On the morning of November 11, 1918, Granddad and his company crossed the River Meuse near Stenay, France, and liberated the village.

At the ceremony for the ninetieth anniversary of the Meuse-Argonne Offensive, on September 26, 2008, the image of General John J. Pershing was projected onto the Montfaucon Monument in Montfaucon, France. The local people refer to it as Pershing's Tower.

Nov. 24th: We left Stenay early and marched out of France [and] in to Belgium about 3 o'clock p.m. And about sundown we got to a small town by the name of Grouville where my pal and I got to bed and had a real good nights sleep. These hikes were sure awful—30 Kilos. [18.64 miles].

THE MARCH TO GERMANY

DURING THE BRIEF TIME BETWEEN THE ARMISTICE AND THE MARCH TO GERMANY, the men got what they needed the most—a rest. Except for eight days, the 89th Division had been under fire since August 4 (more than two months prior) and had taken part in the two largest American battles of the war. The 353rd Infantry Regiment was stationed in Stenay, where they were able at long last to take baths, get deloused, and receive new clothes. To stay busy, the men were organized to clean up Stenay.

Under the terms of the Armistice, the German Army was to evacuate immediately all occupied territory in France, Belgium, and Luxembourg, and to return to Germany across the Rhine River. The Allies began to push the German Army eastward on November 17.[53] The Allied objective was to dismantle the German war machine. A few days later, on November 24, the 89th Division left for Germany and began its march across southern Belgium and Luxembourg. The selected divisions considered it an honor to be included in the occupation forces. The 89th Division Book boasts, "The flower of the American forces was of course chosen for this duty."[54]

They were marching through Belgium when they paused for Thanksgiving Day. Granddad's diary entry for November 25 reads: "One of the boys bought a chicken for his thanksgiving dinner. I had tomatoes, [canned] corn beef, and hard tack for mine. His chicken cost 30 francs, some price." After marching through southern Belgium, they continued on across the tiny country of Luxembourg. On the eastern side of Luxembourg they entered the town of Echternach.

MY JOURNEY TO ECHTERNACH, LUXEMBOURG

My life brightened the day I met Jack Port. It was a few days before June 6 (D-Day), 2007, in Normandy, France, when I first met Jack, who was a 4th Division, D-Day Veteran of Utah Beach. He went all through World War II and experienced some 100 days of combat. He is an American hero. As we started to get to know each other, I told him about my project of following Granddad's diary and that, after D-Day, I was going to drive to eastern France to photograph places where Granddad had been. I mentioned I would also be going through Echternach, Luxembourg. He exclaimed, "Echternach, why, that is where I was during the Battle of the Bulge! Our infantry regiment (the 12th) was surrounded just west of Echternach for four days."

I had been to Echternach twice before and knew that the old Roman bridge Granddad and the 89th Division had used to cross the Sauer River into Germany must have been demolished by the German Army as it retreated during World War II. So I asked Jack if he remembered anything about the bridge. He said he did not but that I needed "to see Fred Karen in Echternach; he's the World War II historian for that whole area. I've been back there several times and I know him well. When I get home, I'll email you his phone number."

Thanks to Jack, I was in Fred Karen's home a few weeks later. I sat on his couch as he showed me his book, *Kriegsereignisse im Fronterktor der Untersauer* (*War Events in the Frontier of the Lower Sauer*). On page 549, there it was, a photo of the demolished bridge taken in February 1945! The key to the photographs (December 1918, February 1945, and today) is the statue of the monk in the middle of the bridge. It seems miraculous that the statue survived the dynamite blasts during the waning months of World War II.

This historic photograph (photographer unknown) of the Echternach Bridge, in early December 1918, records the site where the 89th Division crossed the Sauer River from Luxembourg into Germany. Granddad crossed with his company on December 6. Notice the statue of the monk in the middle of the bridge.[55]

This historic photograph (photographer unknown) of the Echternach Bridge was taken in February 1945, after the German army had dynamited the bridge during its retreat into Germany. Notice that the statue of the monk survived. Used by permission of Fred Karen.[56]

Originally built by the Romans, the Echternach Bridge spans the Sauer River, which defines the border between Luxembourg and Germany. On December 5–6, 1918, the 89th Division crossed this bridge into Germany for the Allied occupation.

Nov. 25th: *Left early again for Germany had a hard hike. Got to a small town named Bisouil [Bezenol] where fourteen of us were in one little room. Here we did a bunch of guard duty, along some of the roads where I put in my time walking patrols, on Ethel's birthday. One of the boys bought a chicken for his thanksgiving dinner. I had tomatoes, corn beef, and hard tack for mine. His chicken cost 30 francs, some price.*

Nov. 30th: *We left this town and went to a town names Foush [Foushes], here we stayed at a place where an old man lived.*

Dec. 2nd: *Got to Noerdauge, stayed here one night.*

Dec. 3rd: *Got to Nommern last town in Belgium.*

Dec 4th: *We were in Beaufort, Luxembourg.*

Dec. 6th: *We went in to Germany at eleven o'clock. We crossed the Sauer River at Echternach. From here we passed through a number of towns including Pittbourg [Bitburg] and on Dec 7th, we reached a farm where we all stayed in a barn one night.*

Occupation of Germany

The 89th Division's task during the occupation was to guard the rail line between Trier and Prüm, Germany. The 353rd Infantry Regiment secured the northern rail section and spent most of the occupation in or near the town of Prüm. During the Christmas season of 1918, Granddad and a small number of his company were billeted with families in the village of Philippsheim.

Years ago, my mother told me Granddad's 1918 Christmas story. He and his pal, Walter Spencer, stayed only a few days with a family in the village. On Christmas Eve, he and his friend talked it over and decided they should leave for a few hours so that the family could celebrate Christmas by themselves. So they went for a walk and most likely saw other friends in their unit. After some time had passed, they returned home and found the family patiently waiting for them, so they could all have Christmas together. After four years of a world gone mad, some semblance of humanity had been restored.

Walking through the tiny village (maybe fifteen homes) of Philippsheim during late June 2007, I was thirsty and went into a small, single-story inn to see if I could get a bottle of water. Inside the lobby, a friendly fellow in his mid-twenties stood up from behind the desk and asked if there was anything I needed. I told him, and he gave me a glass of water. As I drank, he asked in excellent English, "What brings you to Philippsheim?" I told him the Christmas story. "Oh my God, you need to meet Grandpa Johann!" he said with great excitement. He took me through the kitchen of his home and out into the backyard, and there was ninety-two-year-old Grandpa Johann, chopping firewood. With electric enthusiasm, the grandson told the Christmas story to his grandpa in German. Grandpa Johann's eyes became as big as saucers, and he hurriedly replied. Translating, the grandson told me what he had said: "My parents told me that when I was very little, American soldiers stayed in our home over Christmas!" I was astounded, and so were they. We'll never know if it really was the same home in which Granddad stayed, but it was certainly close enough for the three of us. Old Johann then went on with other fascinating stories.[57] Meeting Grandpa Johann was a special moment, as he was the only person I met on my journey whom Granddad may have also met during his time in Europe.

Ninety-two-year-old Grandpa Johann,
in whose parents' home Granddad and
his friend, Walter, may have been billeted
during Christmas 1918, when Johann
was just a baby.

Granddad's diary ends on February 5, 1919, so I have relied on his 353rd Regimental Book to piece together the rest of his time in Europe. In typical army fashion, the young men were kept busy with constant drills and marching. As the spring of 1919 approached, however, the army organized short excursions for the men, so they could enjoy some of the sites of Europe. I know that Granddad joined two such trips. The first was by train to Koblenz, Germany, where they boarded a boat, sailed up the Rhine River, and saw the vineyards and castles of the Rhine Valley. Granddad recounted carving the initials of his girlfriend in the mast of the boat (though I'm not sure whether they were the initials of a girl back home or a German *fräulein*). The second trip was to Lake Annecy in eastern France near the Swiss border. This was another trip by train from Prüm. As evidenced by a receipt from a shop in Annecy, I know that Granddad attended this trip and purchased a clock for his sister, Anna.

The 89th Division marched through this valley in the German countryside, just northeast of the Echternach Bridge, on the way north to Prüm, and Trier, Germany.

Dec. 8th: *The next day was Sunday and was supposed to be a day of rest but very little rest we got. In [the] first place, there wasn't much to eat so my pal and I went to a small town to get something to eat. We got some apples, and went [when] we got back the order came to move to St. Thomas where we were to guard the railroad. We found our way to Killybourg [Kylburg] an[d] as we got a late start. This was Division HQ. From here we started to find St. Thomas but got lost and had to get a Dutchman to lead the way. Got here 1 a.m. the morning of the 9th of Dec. some h--- of a hike too.*

Dec. 19th, 11 A.M.: *We moved to Philippsheim, w[h]ere we still guarded railroads. Here I spent Christmas with [a] Dutch [German] family. Spencer and I each had a bed and a room together just fine.*

January 5th: We got orders to move and were relived by the 340th Art.[artillery] and we got up at 5 a.m. and went to Splicer [Speicher] where we got paid, and waited for a freight train to take us to Prum [Prüm]. We got this train at 12:40 p.m. and rode till dark.

Granddad crossed over the Kyll River using this railroad bridge near Speicher, Germany, on a northbound freight train on January 5, 1919, during the Allied occupation of Germany.

Jan. 5th, [1919]: *We got orders to move and were relived by the 340th Art. and we got up at 5 a.m. and went to Splicer [Speicher] where we got paid, and waited for a freight train to take us to Prum. We got this train at 12:40 p.m. and rode till dark.*

Jan. 6th: *Then we got to Prum [Prüm] and had some hike in the rain and the wind to a small place called Fleruger [Fleringen] where we stayed for a long time and had plenty of drill.*

Jan. 10th: *I got a pass and went to Prum [Prüm]. The first pass I have had since I am over here.*

Jan. 13th: *I shaved (the moustache) off my upper lip, which I started some time after the St. Mihiel drive.*

Jan. 14th: *The Company went to Prum [Prüm] to get deloused and got a bath. This was the start of getting rid of the cooties. About 9 kilos hike. Made it all in four hours hike and bath. Jan. 14th Vanna and I had a chicken, the first I had eaten in the [this] part of the world. He and I ate one alone the next two nights. We had the same, they cost us ten Mark[s] each.*

Feb. 5th: *Left Fleirugen [Fleringen] and came to a little town near Prum [Prüm] called Neiderprüm. Left Flernger [Fleringen] [at] noon and arrived at Niederprüm 3 a.m. the same day. From the fifth of Jan. to about the fifteen of Feb. is when we had the coldest weather.*

The village of Fleringen, Germany is located just east of Prüm, where Granddad and his company were billeted in private homes during the month of January 1919.

Homeward Bound

"It is with pride in our success that I extend my sincere thanks for your splendid service to the army and to the nation."[58]

—General John J. Pershing

Before returning home, each division was personally thanked by General Pershing, whose final inspection of the 89th Division took place on April 23, 1919. For this farewell, the entire division assembled for the first time in Europe at an airfield near General Pershing's headquarters in Trier. On May 4, the 353rd Regiment assembled in Prüm to be decorated by the French government. This was the final tribute to the regiment on foreign soil. A French Army Corps commander fixed the *Croix du Guerre* pennant to the regimental flag.

On May 6, the 353rd Regiment began leaving Prüm for Brest, France, in trains made up of forty cars of the usual *hommes-chevaux* type that carried 40 men or 8 horses. Located in Brittany, at France's westernmost point of land, Brest served as a major American supply port during the war. Granddad and his Company A were on the last train that left for Brest on the evening of May 7. Their mission completed, they boarded the troopship USS Leviathan on the morning of May 13 and set sail for New York City the following evening. As the French coastline faded below the horizon, Granddad and his fellow doughboys must have felt a great sense of accomplishment. They had helped to end the war and their efforts were believed to have yielded a lasting peace. After all, it was supposed to be the "war to end all wars."

My goal in this book has been to use Granddad's diary to connect with a bygone era that still has relevance for today's fast-paced world. I have seen how he and so many brave Americans walked on the world stage at a critical time in history. During the War, 80,894 brave Americans died, 35,373 of which remain in eight American cemeteries in France, Belgium, and England.[59] The profound contributions of the doughboys saved democratic freedom, and we owe them our gratitude by keeping their memory alive. Granddad spent eleven months in Europe, and those eleven months shaped his life, America's destiny, and world history for the twentieth century and beyond.

The Naval Monument in Brest, France, commemorates the achievements of the U.S. Navy during World War I [60].

Afterword

This panorama shows the site where Archduke Franz Ferdinand was assassinated, in Sarajevo, Bosnia. The corner of the three-story building at left is the infamous site, and the Latin Bridge is in the foreground.

opposite: Today, the brown-colored building at the Assassination Corner is a museum; in 1914, it was the Moritz Shiller delicatessen.

Dᴜʀɪɴɢ ᴍʏ ᴛʀɪᴘꜱ ᴛᴏ Eᴜʀᴏᴘᴇ to study and photograph sites of World War I, I had not been to the fateful street corner in Sarajevo, Bosnia, where the Great War began. So, in late June 2013, curiosity took me to the exact place where the Archduke Franz Ferdinand was assassinated on June 28, 1914. This cataclysmic incident was the flashpoint, the spark that ignited the inferno. So I photographed the assassination site on the ninety-ninth anniversary at the same time of day it happened, at 10:30 a.m.

As I stood staring at this dull, unremarkable corner, I thought of the interconnectivity of our world and could scarcely imagine how a local event in a remote corner of Europe could have caused my grandfather to go to war from Denver, Colorado. It seemed a gigantic step—or was it? When the war started my grandfather was nineteen years old, working at the Park Hill Floral Company and taking the trolley to Elitch Gardens Trocadero Ballroom for weekend dances. How different can two worlds possibly be? Three years and nine months later, Granddad went to war. The contorted path of history that swept him into the conflict is astonishing.

WORLD WAR I CEMETERIES IN EUROPE [61]

	Graves	Missing	Combined
Brookwood (England)	468	563	1,031
Flanders Field (Belgium)	368	43	411
Somme (France)	1,844	333	2,177
Aisne-Marne (France)	2,289	1,060	3,349
Oise-Aisne (France)	6,012	241	6,253
Meuse-Argonne (France)*	14,246	954	15,200
St. Mihiel (France)	4,153	284	4,437
Suresnes (Paris, France)**	1,541	974	2,515
Total	**30,921**	**4,452**	**35,373**

* Includes some of the Missing from the expedition to Northern Russia, 1918-19
** There are 24 WWII Dead buried as Unknowns, which are not included in the total number of graves

THE AMERICAN BATTLE MONUMENTS COMMISSION (ABMC) was established by the U.S. Congress in 1923, at the request of General John J. Pershing, to commemorate the service and sacrifice of the American armed forces. The ABMC currently manages twenty-five overseas military cemeteries and twenty-six memorials, monuments, and markers. Most of the cemeteries and monuments honor those who served in both world wars.

There are eight American military World War I cemeteries in Europe—one in England, one in Belgium, and six in France—for a combined total of 30,921 graves and 4,452 names engraved on the Walls of the Missing.[62] Not all deaths were a result of combat, as accidents, illness, and disease, especially influenza, also took a heavy toll. Every family had a choice of having its loved ones buried in Europe or brought home. According to the ABMC, roughly sixty percent of America's military dead from both World War I and World War II were brought home for internment. In addition, there are twelve American World War I monuments and two brass plaques markers in Europe. These plaques were installed to commemorate army headquarters buildings. Many of the monuments are paired with specific cemeteries.

1. As quoted in Louis Untermeyer, *Modern American Poetry* (New York: Harcourt, Brace and Howe, 1919), passim.

2. John J. Pershing, "Our National War Memorials in Europe," *National Geographic Magazine* (January 1934): 36. Pershing's full quote is as follows: "To the other Gold Star Mothers, to relatives of soldier dead, and to every American citizen, I can give assurance that the United States Government has kept and will continue to maintain its trust in perpetuating the memory of the bravery and sacrifices of our World War heroes. Time will not dim the glory of their deeds."

3. Winston Churchill, *The World Crisis*, 6 vols.(New York: Scribner's Sons, 1923–1931): *passim*.

4. "Still in the grip of the Great War," *The Economist* (March 29, 2014): 87.

5. The area between the Allied army front lines and the German army's front lines was known as "no man's land."

6. George H. English, *History of the 89th Division 1917, 1918, 1919* (Denver, Co: Smith-Brooks Printing Company, The War Society of the 89th Division, 1920), 49.

7. Ibid, 50.

8. Captain B. H. Liddell Hart, *The Real War*, 1914–1918 (Boston, MA: Little, Brown, and Company, 1930; revised, 1964)

9. Barbara W. Tuchman, *The Zimmermann Telegram* (New York: Random House Publishing Group, 1994), 7.

10. Ibid, 199.

11. Byron Farwell, *Over There: The United States in the Great War, 1917–1918* (New York: W. W. Norton & Company, Inc., 1999), 35.

12. Camp Funston was named after General Funston.

13. General Pershing had been nicknamed 'Black Jack' because of his early service on the American western frontier with the all-black 10th Cavalry.

14. Farwell, *Over There*, 38.

15. John Keegan, *The First World War* (New York: Vintage Books, 1999), 373.

16. In Basic Training, the men were assigned to numerical companies.

17. A World War I United States Army company consisted of 256 officers and men.

18. American Battle Monuments Commission, *American Armies and Battlefields in Europe* (Arlington, VA: American Battle Monuments Commission, 1938), 31.

19. Barbara W. Tuchman, *The Guns of August* (New York: Macmillan, 1962), 141.

20. Keegan, *The First World War*, 185.

21. English, *History of the 89th Division*, 89.

22. Carlo D'Este, *Patton: A Genius For War* (New York: Harper Perennial, 1996), 230.

23. An army is a collection of two or more corps, and a corps is a collection of two or more divisions. A division was comprised of 27,000 troops divided into four Infantry regiments.

24. Farwell, *Over There*, 210.

25. Ibid, 215.

26. In Denver, Colorado, the American Legion Post One is named in his honor.

27. American Battle Monuments Commission internal archives.

28. After a ceremony, the French people host a reception called the *Vin d'honneur* or the "wine of honor."

29. On September 21, 2013, I talked with Remi Bécourt Foch, and he explained his genealogy.

30. Martin Gilbert, *The First World War* (New York: Henry Holt and Company, 1994), 459.

31. John J. Pershing, *Final Report of General John J. Pershing* (Washington, DC: Washington Government Printing Office, 1920), 43.

32. The eternal flame at the French Tomb of the Unknown Soldier (*Tombe du Soldat inconnu*) is underneath the Arc de Triomphe in Paris and was originally lit by the Sacred Flame in Verdun. The Unknown French soldier is also from the Battle of Verdun.

33. Jim Lacey, *Pershing* (New York: Palgrave Macmillan, 2008), 159.

34. Douglas Mastriano went on to receive a Ph.D. in history, specializing in World War I, with an emphasis in the Meuse-Argonne Offensive. He is now a colonel and Professor of Military Strategy at the U.S. Army War College.

35. Douglas Mastriano is a leading authority on Sergeant York's story. He is responsible for the memorial at the site that was dedicated on the Sergeant York 90th Anniversary (August 8, 2008) by three descendents of Sergeant Alvin York (son, George York; grandson, Gerald York; and great-granddaughter, Deborah York.) Mastriano's son, Josiah, along with the Boy Scouts of America, developed the walking trail to the memorial. Mastriano has written a book about Sergeant York.

36. Robert H. Ferrell, *America's Deadliest Battle, Meuse-Argonne, 1918* (Lawrence: University Press of Kansas, 2007), 76.

37. Farwell, *Over There*, 312.

38. Ferrell, *America's Deadliest Battle*, 78.

39. Farwell, *Over There*, 310.

40. Ferrell, *America's Deadliest Battle*, 84.

41. Ibid, 148.

42. Farwell, *Over There*, 234.

43. English, *History of the 89th Division*, 152.

44. Lacey, *Pershing*, 170.

45. Ferrell, *America's Deadliest Battle*, 131.

46. Farwell, *Over There*, 239.

47. English, *History of the 89th Division*, 170.

48. Ferrell, *America's Deadliest Battle*, 132.

49. The Archduke Franz Ferdinand was assassinated on June 28, 1914, which began a domino effect that started World War I.

50. Lacey, *Pershing*, 4.

51. In 1954, President Eisenhower signed legislation that changed Armistice Day to Veterans Day.

52. Although he goes by Charlie, his full name is Robert C. Slosson. He was then a major and, in June 2012, he was promoted to lieutenant colonel.

53. American Battle Monuments Commission, *American Armies and Battlefields*, 488.

54. English, *History of the 89th Division*, 253.

55. Ibid, 262. U.S. Army Signal Corps, Photograph #40650 (December 5, 1918).

56. Fred Karen, *Kriegsereignisse im Fronterktor der Untersauer, September 1944—März 1945* (Druck: Sankt-Paulus-Druckerei A.G. Luxembourg, 1989), 549.

57. Johann Neitzert went on to say that the Americans left behind a horse-drawn, wooden water-wagon. When he was a boy, one of his village chores was to lead the horse with the wagon down to a spring. He would fill a bucket and then climb up on to the wagon and pour out the bucket into the opening on top and do this until the tank was full. He said the village used the wagon for many years. He was not at all fond of the water-wagon. During World War II, he was a Werhrmacht infantryman on the Eastern Front. As the war in Europe came to a close in early May 1945, he said he did everything he could to move westward and escape the wrath of the Russian hoards. He surrendered to the Americans and spent time in a prisoner-of-war camp.

58. Captain Charles F. Dienst, et al., *History of The 353rd Infantry Regiment* (Wichita, KS: The 353rd Infantry Society, 1921), 196.

59. American Battle Monuments Commission, Stone Engraving, Suresnes Cemetery, Paris, France.

60. In 1941, Germany controlled all of France. The U.S. monument was situated on the high ground overlooking the harbor, and the Germans wanted the location for a command bunker. So, on July 4, 1941, they dynamited the monument and built their bunker. In 1958, the American Battle Monuments Commission rebuilt the monument to the original specifications, on top of the bunker.

61. American Battle Monuments Commission, www.abmc.gov, or call 703-696-6897.

62. ABMC's brochure honors our war heroes by capitalizing Dead and Missing, as in "our military Dead" and "names of the Missing."

63. Helen Patton's grandfather, George Smith Patton Jr., was born on November 11, 1885, and named after his grandfather, George S. Patton I, and his father, George S. Patton II. Patton Jr. served in both world wars. In World War I he was, among other roles, commander of the U.S. 1st Brigade, Tank Corps. He led his men into combat at the Battle of Saint-Mihiel and in the Meuse-Argonne Offensive.

Bibliography

American Battle Monuments Commission, *American Armies and Battlefields in Europe* (Arlington, VA: American Battle Monuments Commission, 1938).

American Battle Monuments Commission, *American Memorials and Overseas Military Cemeteries* (Arlington, VA: American Battle Monuments Commission, 2003).

Winston Churchill, *The World Crisis, 6 vols.* (New York: Scribner's Sons, 1923–1931).

Carlo D'Este, *Patton: A Genius For War* (New York: Harper Perennial, 1996).

Captain Charles F. Dienst, First Lieutenant Clifford Chalmer, First Lieutenant Francis Morgan, First Lieutenant Charles O. Gallenkamp, First Lieutenant Lloyd H. Benning, First Lieutenant Harold F. Brown, First Lieutenant Morton S. Bailey, and Second Lieutenant William J. Lee, *History of The 353rd Infantry Regiment* (Wichita, KS: The 353rd Infantry Society, 1921).

George H. English, *History of the 89th Division, 1917, 1918, 1919* (Denver, CO: Smith-Brooks Printing Company, The War Society of the 89th Division, 1920).

Byron Farwell, *Over There: The United States in the Great War, 1917–1918* (New York: W. W. Norton & Company, Inc., 1999).

Robert H. Ferrell, *America's Deadliest Battle, Meuse-Argonne, 1918* (Lawrence: University Press of Kansas, 2007).

Martin Gilbert, *The First World War* (New York: Henry Holt and Company, 1994).

Liddell Hart, Captain B. H., *The Real War*, 1914-1918 (Boston, MA: Little, Brown, and Company, 1930; revised, 1964).

Fred Karen, *Kriegsereignisse im Fronterktor der Untersauer, September 1944–März 1945* (Druck: Sankt-Paulus-Druckerei A.G. Luxembourg, 1989).

John Keegan, *The First World War* (New York: Vintage Books, 1999).

Jim Lacey, *Pershing* (New York: Palgrave Macmillan, 2008).

S.L.A. Marshall, *World War I.* (Boston, MA: Houghton Mifflin and American Heritage, 1992).

John J. Pershing, *Final Report of General John J. Pershing* (Washington, DC: Washington Government Printing Office, 1920).

Joseph E. Persico, *11th Month, 11th Day, 11th Hour Armistice Day, 1918* (New York: Random House, 2004).

Barbara W. Tuchman, *The Zimmermann Telegram* (New York: Random House, 1994).

Barbara W. Tuchman, *The Guns of August* (New York: Macmillan, 1962).

Acknowledgments

W HEN I BOARDED A FLIGHT TO FRANCE in early September 2005, I had Granddad's diary, a map of Europe, and a willing heart. I was ready for a grand adventure. By following my grandfather's footsteps, I have learned a great deal about America's World War I experience, and have seen so many magnificent places. But it is the people I have met along the way who have made this an enduring and relevant story.

A special thanks to my friends in Europe who have helped me over the course of my travels: Helen Patton, Remi Foch, Maurice and Monique Leseur, Delphine Voilemin, Patrick and Marie-Jo Simons, Jean-Paul and Brigitte de Vries, David and Marian Howard, and their sons; James, Charles, and Frederick.

My friends at the American Battle Monuments Commission were a tremendous help. They offered their guidance and shared with me their unparalleled knowledge of the Great War. Sincere thanks to: Max Cleland, Michael Conley, and Tim Nosal from the Arlington, Virginia, office; Steven Hawkins (retired), Walter Franklin III, Charles Hunt, and James Woolsey (retired) from the Paris, France, office; Jacques Adelee (retired), Robert Bell, Michael Coonce, and Nadia Ezz-Eddine from the Saint-Mihiel Cemetery; Phil Rivers (deceased), Jeffrey Aarnio, Scott Desjardins, David Bedford, Jason Blount, Dominique Didot, and Nicholas Raffa from the Meuse-Argonne Cemetery; and Angelo Munsel and Gabrielle Mihaescu from the Suresnes Cemetery.

I want to pay special tribute to Phil Rivers, who retired in 2011 as Superintendent of the Meuse-Argonne Cemetery, and passed away on November 21, 2012. He was my friend and mentor for many years and I owe him my gratitude.

This book could not have become a reality without the help of many talented and dedicated people. I am grateful to them for their enthusiasm, creative ideas, and constant encouragement.

A huge thanks to George F. Thompson, the publisher, and his team, for embracing this book, and to my editorial and creative team for really bringing the book to life: Ryan Greendyk, for his untiring enthusiasm and outstanding writing skills; Carlan Tapp, for his brilliant photo editing, and for teaching me how to use a camera; Deborah Reade, for her excellent mapmaking; Colleen Ryor, for her proofreading; and John Dobson, Ph.D., for his historical review. Thanks to my friend, Roger Verity, for giving me a copy of the *Final Report of General John. J. Pershing* and for the Rand McNally 1918 World War I Map, that we adapted here. A special thanks goes to Joanna Hurley for her editorial vision and for finding the right publisher, and to David Skolkin, for his inspired design.

And, most of all, I want to thank my wife, Annie, for believing in me.

JEFF LOWDERMILK is a writer, photographer, lecturer, and student of World Wars I and II. He has traveled extensively throughout Europe, documenting the path detailed in his grandfather's World War I diary. Jeff is the author of *Saluting America's World War I Heroes*, a historical and dedicatory piece centered around Jeff's experiences at the 87th anniversary of the Armistice. Through beautiful, real-to-life photographs and supplemental historical storytelling, Jeff paints a picture of the thriving community that seeks to honor the sacrifices of our country's war heroes. His photographs have been displayed as a solo exhibit at the National World War I Museum in Kansas City, Missouri, and also were featured in the 2010 Annual Report of the American Battle Monuments Commission. The ABMC has also used his photographs in their presentations to Congress. A passionate and creative storyteller, Jeff leads presentations and lectures around the world that weave together his rich imagery, personal anecdotes, and meticulous historical research. He has presented at the Colorado History Museum, New Mexico History Museum, the headquarters of the New Mexico National Guard in Santa Fe, the New Mexico Air National Guard, at Kirtland Air Force Base in Albuquerque, the National World War I Museum, and the Utah Beach Museum in Normandy, France. He lives in Santa Fe, New Mexico, with his wife, Annie. For more information on Jeff's work and presentations please visit www.jefflowdermilk.com.

HELEN PATTON, a native of Hamilton, Massachusetts, who lives in Reims, France, is the granddaughter of General George S. Patton Jr. and the daughter of Major General George S. Patton IV, the decorated Vietnam War hero.[63] She is the founder of the Patton Foundation in the United States and the Patton Stiftung Sustainable Trust in Saarbrucken, Germany. She works tirelessly to keep the memory of the World War II generation alive and helps soldiers, veterans, and their families.

For more information about Helen's important work, please visit www.thepattonfoundation.org.

About the Book

Honoring the Doughboys: Following My Grandfather's World War I Diary was brought to publication in an edition of 1500 hardcover copies. The text was set in Goudy Old Style, the paper is Garda Silk, 150 gsm, and the book was professionally printed and bound in Canada by Friesens.

Publisher: George F. Thompson
Project Manager: Joanna Hurley, of HurleyMedia, L.L.C.
Book Design & Production: David Skolkin
Writing Editor: Ryan Greendyk
Editorial Assistant: Mikki Soroczak
Photography Editor: Carlan Tapp
Historical Review: John Dobson, Ph.D.
Photograph of World War I Artifacts: Carlan Tapp
Proofing/Editing: Colleen Ryor
Mapmaking: Deborah Reade

Publisher: George F. Thompson
Project Manager: Joanna Hurley, of Hurley Media, L.L.C.
Manuscript Editor: Purna Makaram
Editorial Assistant: Mikki Soroczak
Book Design and Production: David Skolkin

George F. Thompson Publishing, L.L.C.
217 Oak Ridge Circle
Staunton, VA 24401-3511, U.S.A.
www.gftbooks.com

Distributed by International Publishers Marketing
www.internationalpubmarket.com

22 21 20 19 18 17 16 15 14   1 2 3 4 5

The Library of Congress Preassigned Control Number is 2013951577.

ISBN: 978–1–938086–18–2

*page 1: This photograph was taken on a late fall afternoon in the Meuse-Argonne Cemetery in
Romagne-sous-Montfaucon, France, which is managed by the American Battle Monuments Commission.*

*page 2: The 5th Signal Command Color Guard Team of the U.S. Army prepares to enter the ninetieth anni-
versary ceremony of the Meuse-Argonne Offensive in the village of Neuvilly-en-Argonne. On the left is the
American Flag, in the center is the French Flag (Tricolor), and on the right is the flag of the U.S. Army, with
"battle streamers," which represent the command's individual battles fought throughout their history.*